Parenting IS Leadership

A Practical Guide to Raising Great Kids

By
Lorna Hegarty

Parenting IS Leadership – A Practical Guide to Raising Great Kids © 2016 by Lorna Hegarty.

All rights reserved. No part of this book may be reproduced in whole or in part, or stored in a retrieval system, or transmitted in any form or by any means, mechanical, photocopying, recording or otherwise, without written permission of the author and publisher. For information regarding permission, email to: lorna@lchresources.com

Copyright © 2016 by Lorna Hegarty. All rights reserved.

ISBN: 978-1-988317-01-4
Published by LCH Resources Limited

First Edition – January 2008
(Originally published as "A Wealth of Parenting – Things Money Can't Buy)
Second Edition – April 2016
(Originally published as "A Wealth of Parenting – Things Money Can't Buy)

This book is copyrighted to Lorna Hegarty. You can distribute the book with permission from the copyright holder or direct interested parties only. No part of this publication may be reproduced or transmitted without prior permission from the copyright holder. Any person who performs any unauthorized act in relation to this publication may be liable to criminal prosecution and civil claims.

Though all attempts have been made to assure that the information given within this book is accurate, the copyright holder and author assumes no responsibility for any inaccuracies, misinterpretation of the information provided or any missed facts.

This book and the material within is not considered to qualify as professional advice of any sort, whether legal or otherwise. All interpretations and applications of the information provided is the sole responsibility of the reader. It is also the sole responsibility of the reader only, rather than the author or copyright holder, to ensure that any use of this information does not infringe on any laws in the country they may be in at the time of using it.

The copyright holder and author will assume no responsibility or any liability in any form for what you the reader choose to do with the information provided. Any interpreted similarity with any organization, or with persons living or deceased, real or fictitious, is purely coincidental.

Also by Lorna Hegarty

The Seven Essential Practices of Great Leaders

The Wealthy Teen:
A Guide for Parents, Teens, Mentors and Coaches

Contents

Foreword 8
Chapter 1: Where Are You Headed? 15
    Happy Family Principle: A Family Mission Statement 17
Chapter 2: Effective Parenting – A Picture is Worth More Than Words 30
Chapter 3: Disciplining with Creativity 41
    Why Do Children Misbehave? 43
    Parenting Styles 48
    Disciplining through Reprimand 53
    Why Discipline Your Child? 58
    Quiz 61
Chapter 4: Connecting with Love 64
    Traditions 71
    Celebrations 75
    Capturing Important Memories 77
    Express Your Love 79
    Talking and Conversation 82
    Doing Things Together 89
Chapter 5: Self-Esteem, Decoded 96
    How Can Parents Help Repair the Damage? 108
    Teens and Self-Esteem Problems 113
Chapter 6: Building Rapport or Keeping the Lines of Communication Wide Open 118
    Exercises 140
Chapter 7: Handling with Care or Dealing with the Terrifying Teens 143
    Teens and Addiction 155
    Teens and Sexual Awareness 159
    Handling Sadness, Anxiety and Depression in Teens 163
    Other Teen Problems 166
Chapter 8: At the Potter's Wheel 169
    Money Management 172
    Extracurricular Activities 174
    Mind Management 176
    Goal Setting 177
    Time Management 181
    Social Skills 183
    Eating Habits 184
    Happiness Skills 186
Conclusion 189
Post Script 193

Dedication

This book is dedicated to my mother Edith, my father David, and my brothers Kevin and John, who initially taught me about family life. We were quite the team, I appreciate and am grateful for all the lessons.

I also acknowledge, with lots of love, my children, Dru, Matthew and Carly. Their love, humour, support, understanding, and fierce independence taught me how to love, laugh, and not take myself so seriously, and that has helped me become the parent I am today.

Foreword

"Everybody knows how to raise children, except the people who have them."
- P. J. O'Rourke

Oh, yes! More than one person has said something like this — that the only person who is absolutely sure of their parenting skills is a person who has never had any children of their own! We parents have heard more than our share of advice from non-parents, haven't we? Our great aunt, and her suggestions for discipline, our own younger sibling, that knows how she/he will raise their children when they are parents. Well-intentioned as they are, we are more likely to rebel against their advice than follow it.

Parenting Is Tough Work!

It is also full of 'what ifs' and 'buts'. I believe there is a wealth of wisdom in those words. When you are a parent, it doesn't matter if your children are toddlers or married with kids of their own. There are moments when you wonder if you've done a good job. Of course, when everything works out for the best, you know that you can afford to give yourself at least a small pat on the back.

The funny thing is that by the time you feel that you have learned the tricks of the trade, so to speak, your fledgling babies have all grown up and flown the nest. There's no one left to 'parent' anymore! The years in between, when you're trying to do your best, never KNOWING if your best is good enough, you may experience undiluted agony.

I have three children in various experiences of adulthood. With them, and through them, I have learnt a lot. I understand now that the best things about being a parent are the memories of the warm hugs and sloppy, wet kisses your little children plant on you when you least expect it. I see now how my daughter's 'Mommmmmmm' (along with her eye roll), was just her way of asking me to back off. I see how there is a direct correlation between being a Leader and being a Parent.

Today, 37 years into parenthood, I am still learning, and in some instances, still Leading.

Letting Go

For instance, I now know that the toughest part about parenting is to know when to let go! (Then to actually do so…)

I also know that there is more learning on the way as I look excitedly into the dim and hazy future of the grandmother I am to be, when my own children will be donning their 'parent caps'.

I did not know all this when I started out. I was little more than a girl when I had my son, Dru. At 21, most girls my age were still 'testing the waters', so to speak. What I remember most about those difficult early years was that it was incredibly hard – as well as amazingly rewarding – to be a parent.

I had no one to turn to for advice. All my girlfriends were busy with their schooling and careers while I was firmly ensconced in diapers, formula, feeding schedules and baby tantrums, not to mention working on my career and education.

The funny thing is, by the time my friends finally caught up with me, and had become mothers themselves, my sons were in their early years. I found myself becoming a mentor or coach of sorts to them, as my friends asked me for advice on how to deal with their problems. I was the recognized Wise Woman in mothering matters! While that gave me a lot of insight into parenting issues, it also meant, as the 'senior' of my group, that I STILL did not have anyone to compare notes with.

Listening to My Heart

Looking back, I see that during those years, I learned to listen to my heart, and to be mindful of what was going on around me and within me. I also learned to network with other parents so I could get ideas from them. Early on, I realized that each child in the family is different, and each parent would handle issues different ways, and in all situations Leadership was important when dealing with issues. I liked to hear how other parents handled difficult times, so I could apply what I felt comfortable doing, and felt my children had the best chance of responding to. I always knew I was not going to be the perfect parent, and was likely contributing to my children's 'issues' – all those lessons they would be unlearning in their later years – even though I tried to be careful with my words and actions.

When Your Child Pushes You Away

I recall a time when my younger son Matthew was dropped from the soccer team. I knew Matthew was hurting inside though he put up a brave front and shrugged off his pain. My heart went out to him but my little 'boy-man' refused to open up to me. When his friends were outside playing, I could hear Matthew listening to his radio in his bedroom. With a mother's intuition, I knew that inside his room, he would be thinking about the soccer decision. It broke my heart to see my young son carrying the weight of the world on his shoulders. The worst of it was that I couldn't seem to help because Matthew refused to discuss it.

When I could stand it no longer, I went to the soccer grounds, just to watch the other boys play. As I sat there on the bench, not looking at anything in particular, just listening to my heart, a man in his early fifties approached me. He knew Matthew, he said. He had watched him play and he had seen me cheering my son on a number of times. He also knew that Matthew was no longer on the team. We got talking and I found myself spilling all my frustration and Matthew's pain to this stranger. "I don't seem to be getting through to him. He was always an open, communicative child, but now, it's like there is a different person inside him. I want to help him but he pushes me away. I just don't know what to do," I remember saying. The wise reply I received from that soft-spoken father filled my heart, and it stays with me even today. "Oh, you know what to do. In your heart, you know that Matt has to get over his pain in his own way and in his own time. It is just that, as parents, we sometimes feel uncomfortable letting our kids feel their pain. We want to shield them and protect them, even when they really are old enough to handle things. We can't always do that, you know. Let him be. You'll see, Matt will come out of the experience a little wiser than the young boy who left the field."

And he was right. The amazing thing was that this piece of advice made such sense to me at that particular time, that it instantly lifted my spirits and gave me a sense of direction. Now, I felt I knew what to do!

Let Things Be

These and other incidents have taught me that parenthood is all about feeling with your brain and thinking with your heart, particularly when it comes to handling your pre-teens and teens. There is no right or wrong in any situation; there is only what you *feel* is right and what you *think* will work.

I remember telling my boys that I did not have any experience raising children, and that I was going to make some mistakes. I asked them to be patient with me. I wanted them to understand that I was doing my best in each circumstance. I always wanted to keep the channels of communication open. I especially feel this way as I was raising a teenage daughter, which is a first for me (Hint: Raising boys is different from raising girls...).

This book has been a long time in the making. It was first published in 2008, and now I've decided it is time to update the book. I've been learning lessons from my children for the last 37 years of my life. When I finally started to write this book, I was surprised at the rush of thoughts that came into my head, and the fond memories that marked the progress and development of this book. Unconsciously, I had been filing important information away and I now realize that this book was meant to be, and it was time to reflect and update some of the messages.

My family is whom and what I care about the most, and I'm sure you feel the same way. Successful families do not just happen. They require work, patience, practice, discipline, creativity, humor, communication, and even more patience! In this book, I'll be sharing with you some experiences of my family, how we've bungled things, as well as how we've weathered the storms. I will also be sharing with you some of the learning experiences I have been fortunate enough to hear from my wide circle of friends, clients and acquaintances and through my website at www.coachlorna.com

My aim in sharing these stories is not to tell you what is right or wrong, for I know that it is best if we can be observers in our lives, not judges. I know that every situation is unique and that every family has their own circumstances to deal with.

Families these days come in many forms: single parents, divorced and doubled families, blended families, same sex parent families, relatives raising children, and grandparents stepping up to the plate in all kinds of family need. Some of the incidents and explanations may ring a bell; others may leave you cold. There just isn't a One-Size-Fits-All for family matters. Whether you relate to the stories and the experiences in their totality or not, I hope you find yourself connecting with the underlying philosophies and principles.

I hope that the information in this book will help you make the best decisions you can make as a parent for your child or children. Doing the best you can in each circumstance is all that is asked of you. Thoughtful, mindful reflection, before words are spoken or actions are taken are a must, though it is often the hardest thing in the world to remember in the heat of the moment. Also, learning how to deliver a heartfelt apology is a skill, we as parents, and as human beings need to develop.

Finally, and above all else, I want to instill a sense of hope in you. Those teen years and the period on both sides of the difficult teens can be very hard on parents.

Making Better Decisions

I remember reading somewhere that when people are faced with a bad situation at their office or in their company, they toy with the problem and come up with a solution or a new set of decisions to eradicate or resolve the problem. This dynamic problem-solving does not always happen when trouble hits our families. Probably, that is because we are too emotionally involved, or there are no scientific principles that will lead you to a watertight solution. If you take nothing else from this book but the realization that *things will work out when you come from the place of love,* I would consider my work done.

Life Refines You and Relationships Mold You

Families are all about relationships. That is the bottom line. As you strive to develop more and more harmony in all your relationships at home, life refines you into a more harmonious person. Working on those relationships molds you into a more mature, settled person, for whom drama is momentary and problems can all find resolution.

Your greatest contribution as a parent is to teach your children that life does go on, notwithstanding any difficulties in any of your family or outside relationships. However, before you reassure them that they can and will get past the hard times, you have to understand that there is plenty of light at the end of the tunnel, even if you cannot see it right away. Parenting can be fun and it can be a mutually enriching experience, if you let it.

Often, we as parents get far too caught up in little things! As the famous book title says, "Don't sweat the small stuff!"

I hope this book will help you see the bigger picture. I also hope that you will understand that things aren't that bad after all, and you're just one amongst the millions of confused, anxious, worried parents out there. Like I was back in the day and – truth be told – still am at times!

Chapter 1: Where Are You Headed?

"The child supplies the power but the parents have to do the steering."
- Benjamin Spock

As we look around for guidance for ourselves in our role as parents, we eventually have to realize that we are the leader, or Captain of the Ship for our kids.

Children are so energetic and so vital (and today so busy), that we might get caught up in just going along with the current of the waters. But as parents, we need to hold firmly to the rudder, and direct it according to our values, our vision for our family, and our hopes for our kids' futures.

Envisioning

One of the parents I met in Dru's swimming classes was a cheerful man who had an equally cheerful son. This father-son pair never failed to surprise and impress me with their positive vibes, affectionate body language and camaraderie. The young mother that I was, with two rambunctious boys of my own, I made it a point to ask that father what his secret was. Here is what he replied:

> "I've never thought about it much. But now that you ask me, I think it's just that *I envisioned my family as my best friends.* To me, they are the people I feel most at home with. You know, I have a picture on my living room wall that reads 'Home Sweet Home'. That's one of my favorite objects in our house. I guess I

may have really internalized that because my home is the sweetest place for me."

He went on to explain that he had another son who had passed away years earlier with a childhood disease, and after getting out of a deep depression, he chose to cherish the relationship he could have with the son he had left to raise. This unfortunate premature death had given the father a cause to reflect on his values, and he approached every day as a wonderful day that held the chance to connect with his family. He told me that he had down moments, as anyone does, and when they were upon him, he practiced envisioning what's right in his life as opposed to what was not right! His goal was to focus his attention on the best possible relationship he could have with his son, and he took it day by day, as that was all he knew he could focus on.

Did you notice the key word here? "*Envisioned*"! The crux of a happy family life lies in that one word. This man was able to have such a winning relationship with his family because he had a clear *vision* of the type of family he wanted. Consciously and unconsciously (for both aspects of being are always operational), he was working towards the picture on his wall.

Human beings have an acute sense of direction and we are happiest when we're moving towards a predefined goal. We rarely venture out without a destination in mind. Most of us even have the route in our heads before we get into the car. The same applies to work: we have daily tasks to complete and also weekly, monthly, quarterly and yearly targets. Targets are wonderful things; they tell us what our final destination is. They make us think of our route and set certain guidelines for our travel. They ensure that we reach our destination even if we lose the way or get a little delayed.

When you stop and think about it, isn't it strange that most families have no sense of destination?

Imagine, here we are in the greatest and the most enriching experience of our lives and we have no clear-cut goals or end in mind. Have you ever thought where your family would be 10 years, 5 years or even 5 months from now? How about starting with the goal for the day? Have you ever asked yourself:

What is it that I want from – and with – my family?

Happy Family Principle: A Family Mission Statement

One of the most important principles of a loving, fun-filled family? Working towards a common goal.

Perhaps you want your children to develop healthy eating habits. Or you want everyone to learn responsibility by lending a helping hand with the chores at home. You may want your children to stop fighting with each other and follow the rules you've set down. Maybe, like most parents, you hold a mental picture of the perfect family in your head and your current reality makes you cringe.

- ➢ Do you feel that your children are just an assorted bunch of snarling, loud, messy, contentious people moving in and out of each other's lives due to compulsion and convenience … rather than affection and loyalty?

- ➢ Are your family relationships leaving you unsatisfied, unfulfilled and uncomfortable … rather than comforted and happy?

- ➢ Do you dream of having the same kind of warm and fulfilling relationships with your children that you had with your parents and siblings when you were young … rather than the free-for-all you may have now?

If you can relate to any of the above, rest assured: you're not alone. In fact, you would be surprised to know that many parents all over the world feel the same way. Each one of us dreams of having the perfect family. We want everything to be perfect, just as we see in the movies. We want loving relationships, happy and balanced children, peace and happiness, and perhaps enough money in the bank. When we sense the gap between what we want and what we actually have, we can feel hopeless, frustrated and depressed.

>   Every family is unique. The family changes with the introduction of each new child that is born to it, as well as when each of the children hit different ages and stages in their growth. There are evolutionary milestones, so to speak, which require all of us in the family to gently adapt.

A Family Shares Values

You have your own values – ethics, guiding principles, personal standards, and beliefs – which you have developed along your life path, and pass these on overtly or covertly to your children. Children copy us, for better or for worse.

For some families, values create a drive towards achievements like higher education. For others, values are what lead us to share a simpler, more laid back, and perhaps more fun-filled life. For still others, values lead us to pitch in when the greater community needs help (think volunteering at a food bank, taking a cooked meal to a family in crisis, driving someone to an appointment).

What are your values? Do you have relationship resolutions or goals?

It is important to identify what drives you and your family because shared values can become one of the most powerful and cohesively binding forces in your family. Shared values create a mindful understanding about how life works, and what our role is, not only in the family but out in the world. Values can override the pain of past miseries and give your family the strength to survive the daily challenges of life. They can help you become a supportive, proactive and balanced parent while keeping your children on the path of your choice, and of their choice as well. As children grow and make decisions for themselves, they learn to make the correct choices based on the values you have taught them.

Let me remind you of an interesting game that some children play, and indeed formed part of my recess when in junior school years. We would form big human chains and run behind a person. As soon as that person is caught, he or she joins the chain and the chain grows larger and larger. Half the fun of the game is to 'recruit' more people into the chain and keep it growing. What made the game so much fun was that the bigger the chain, the more effective it was IF and WHEN every member ran towards a single goal. When that happened, the 'victim' had no choice; he or she had nowhere to run and getting caught was only a matter of time.

You could think of this chain as being composed of your family members. It might not be that big, but you cannot function if various members are pulling in different directions. To move forward, you have to take all of them along. To do that, you need their consent, participation and wholehearted approval regarding the values and goals you have chosen. How do you achieve this?

> *You must first identify your common values and figure out how to have every person in the family 'commit' himself/herself to achieving a shared success.*

Family Is a 'We' Movement, not an 'I' or 'You' Movement

One of the things I remember about my childhood was the way my Mom would react to food left on the plate. She would get very upset. Back in her own younger days, the rule was that you ate all food on your plate, no questions asked.

We kids always wondered what the big fuss was about. Mom made it a point that we eat what we were served, whether it was brussel sprouts, broccoli, lima beans or carrots. If we did not eat what was on our plate, we would spend hours just sitting and looking at the food, as we were not going to be excused from the table. If we ever managed to slip the veggies into the trashcan, or throw them behind the fridge (I'm serious...) we could be sure that mom would find out. At one point, there was such anger and tears about the food situation, that mom suggested we sit down and talk about what we could do to resolve the problem.

That was my first taste of negotiation. Mom told us, firstly, that she had concerns and real fears of nutrition, and balanced eating. Secondly, she also wanted us to respect food, as it was not plentiful everywhere in the world and, as such, we should not waste it.

We, my brothers, Kevin, John, and I, told her that we would happily pay for the shipping of the food to other countries if it meant we were not going to have to eat it. Needless to say, that was not the reaction my mother was looking for! Actually if I recall correctly, that got me a few hours of 'bench' time. It seemed like the classic situation of an immovable force meeting an indestructible object. She wouldn't budge and neither would we. We would not agree to eat veggies we did not like.

The next day, mom was home early from work. She was up in her room doing something mysterious. After dinner and the usual fuss, mom called us all to her room. She had made a colorful chart that listed the nutrient values of all the veggies we didn't like. On the other side, she had listed the values of the junk food we were always happy to eat. At the bottom, she had written in bright red:

"Family Food Correction Mission:
*To eat **more** of these (pointing to veggies)*
*and to eat **less** of these (pointing to the sweets)"*

She told us that this was going to be our goal. Then she asked us to come up with a way to fulfill this goal!

Ah, the power of being allowed to input to decision-making!

We felt so good about the <u>responsibility</u> of being asked to resolve the problem, that we earnestly threw ideas back and forth until we hit upon a solution. We decided that we'd have a medley of those veggies once a week. On these nights, we would be given a treat; it could be anything we liked. It was an incentive for getting through the disliked veggies.

And you know, it worked. We knew that every Wednesday was *"Vile Veggies"* night and we submitted ourselves to it because we loved the home made treacle toffee or the fruit shakes we'd get afterwards. Dinnertimes were a huge rush to devour every bit of the disliked veggies from our plates! I don't know how she came up with her idea, but looking back, I see that mom was one smart lady! I remember that chart even today.

Notice how my mom showed leadership by turning this ugly situation into a win-win scenario, with a little innovative thinking? Instead of inflicting her will on us, she decided to make healthy eating a family goal. Then she went a step further and gave us the much-needed sense of participation. We *had to* find the way towards the goal. We felt empowered, and we *chose* to participate.

Interestingly, today there are not any veggies I don't enjoy eating...

Develop Your Family Mission Statement

A Family Mission Statement is an unbreakable vow that we make to the members of our family.

It is a statement of commitment. A call to positive action. A binding agreement on all those who contributed towards making it.

When created with love and dedication, your family's mission statement can become the most defining aspect of your family life.

To come up with a Family Mission Statement, ask these questions of yourself and your family:

- → What do you want to be important in your family?
- → What words or phrases mean something to your family?
- → How do you want to treat each other and be treated?
- → What makes your family happy?
- → What things do your family do really well together?
- → How will you remember your Family Mission Statement?
- → What values do you hold regarding education, charity work, discipline, lifestyle, digital/TV time, phone use, family time, extracurricular activities for children, spending / investing / saving money, etc.?
- → What values do you share regarding tolerance and respect of others' ways of living?

Mutual understanding and trust in the home is the beginning of harmony. It is the beginning of the 'we' relationship I wrote about earlier. When you share and agree on your expectations, vision, values and problem-solving strategies, you bind together more firmly. Your sense of direction becomes clearer and more focused.

Examples in My Family

A value we strongly wanted in our family was love. We, as a family, thought that the image of hearts would best remind us to love each other, to be kind to each other and not say mean words to each other. We decorated our kitchen with hearts from one end to the other, and top to bottom! We had heart wallpaper, heart curtains, and even heart cups to drink from. It was always nice to eat in the kitchen surrounded by hearts. The children used to make drawings of hearts to put on the fridge, and when we were looking for gifts for special occasions for each other, many times it would incorporate the heart theme! To this day, all three of my children remember the heart theme in the kitchen when they were growing up.

Clarity within Your Couple

When my daughter Carly was young, we used to take her shopping with us. I still remember the pretty picture she made running excitedly from one aisle to the other in the supermarket as we followed behind her. She would see something that excited her in every aisle. She would then ask us to buy a little of this, a few of that, and some of those. Her father and I started to notice that if one of us said 'no' to her request, she would ask the other to see if there would be a different answer.

When my husband and I sat down alone to discuss the pattern that we had started to experience, we talked about our values, how we were treated in our families, how we treated ourselves and how that made us who we are today. We were able to come to some interesting conclusions, and to develop a plan of action.

The discussion led us to a common approach. We told Carly that we would not buy something for her every time we went to the store. When we decided that it would be fine for her to pick something, it would just be one item from the whole store. We would decide before going to the store whether she would be buying something on that particular trip or not. If she was, we then discussed the amount we were willing to pay. Carly also had allowance and that was factored into shopping. She now understood the rules, and it was clear that she could not get away with playing one parent against the other. Even today, she remains a joy to shop with as she does not get cranky if she asks me to buy something and I say 'no' ... or if she has to deny herself a purchase because she doesn't want to break into her savings!

When BOTH parents share a common vision, your couple's sense of purpose becomes more concrete. You know what you are working toward. You do not step on each other's feelings inadvertently and you cement a stronger relationship, and show leadership.

Then, when the children come along, you automatically act as a single unit. If there are things you disagree on, discuss them in private. Once you have a clear direction, a discussion with the rest of the family can take place. It is important for parents to follow this pattern and support each other.

It is also important for parents to model a method of discussing differences. This is how children learn to relate to others. This sets them up for successful relationships with their partners and peers later on in life. They learn that you say what you mean, and mean what you say. It can be extra stressful as a single parent when all the responsibility for decisions sit with you. In most cases, I found it necessary <u>not</u> to change the very important rules we had agreed upon, as it confused the children. It is perfectly fine to revisit the rules, however, if you had good reasons for making them, and not great reasons for breaking them, chances are, the behavior you had gotten them away from, will pop right back into your reality. Children will notice that when they push hard enough, you give in.

Involve the Kids

Back to the Mission Statement! The next step in building your Mission Statement is to get your children involved in the process.

When children are young, they are more forthcoming about their expectations and fears. At younger ages, they contribute freely and love to be included in the process. Also, it is a wonderful experience for young children to know that their feelings and opinions are important.

As children grow older, their open contribution to a family mission statement may not be spontaneous. Sometimes, they will come out with hurtful or annoying statements: "Oh, just leave me alone, will you?" or "Can we do this some other time, I have a school assignment, you know" or the most irritating of them all "I need to check my email. You go ahead, I'm OK with whatever you decide"!

These things happen and all you can do is keep going with a smile plastered on your face. "No, dear, email will have to wait". One father told me that he had to rope in his teen daughter's cooperation by offering a small bribe.

> "I promised that she could watch her favorite show without sharing TV time with me for a week – usually we swap channels and we squabble over it. She grabbed the chance, as I knew she would. It was worth missing my favorite game to see my daughter coming out with her ideas and connecting with us like she used to when she was young.
>
> Besides, at the end of the week, she even told me that she missed our little squabbles over the remote control!"

I have spent many years without a TV in our home, so I have not been able to use that as a negotiating tool with my children! Bribes can be a good thing, when used thoughtfully! Of course, don't go buying your teenager a car if they keep their room clean... A small treat to acknowledge their change of behavior may be appropriate.

Bribes I have used: a trip to get an ice cream from a favorite ice cream parlor on the other side of town; their choice of restaurant for a one-on-one breakfast; a walk to buy a magazine at the bookstore. My bribes usually involve doing something with the child, not just buying them something.

Before you start your discussions on a Family Mission statement, tell everyone to gather around and be prepared to "talk family." Here are some preparatory considerations:

- Have colorful pens, paper, magazines, and perhaps some healthy treats ready.
- Young children may want to cut out pictures of a 'happy family' or a heart for love, which helps them out if they can't read. The pictures will represent what is important in your family, and what you are going to remember when the going gets tough.
- Young children have short attention spans, so be prepared to keep it short and fun-filled.
- Older children usually prefer longer and more complicated interactions once they get into the mood. A ten-minute session with older children will only make them feel that you are not interested in hearing them out.
- If any of the children resist, you might want to spend some private time with them and find out what they want from/in the family.

A mother once told me that her adolescent stepson refused to participate in family discussions because he felt uncomfortable with her three daughters crowding him out. He felt outnumbered. Talking privately with him made her understand how he felt. With acknowledgement to his feelings, and some rules about equal participation, he eventually participated.

When you finally get everyone to sit down at the table and you begin your discussion, make the Ground Rules clear:

- Every one speaks in turns and everybody listens to everyone else respectfully.
- Write down ALL the points that are made, as it confirms that every person has contributed. Be sure you acknowledge each contribution!

- ➢ Summarize what each person has said so you can verify whether you have understood correctly.
- ➢ Don't judge any contribution. There is potential in any contribution.

It often happens that at the end of the discussion, there are too many suggestions in front of you. You cannot realistically get all of them into your mission statement. The next step is to remove those things that are of less importance – with everyone's consent. Now that you have all the points on paper, sit down and write out a mission statement.

Here are some guidelines to writing an effective and inspiring mission statement:

- ➢ Make it fun
- ➢ Make it simple – really simple if the children are young
- ➢ Make it easy to remember
- ➢ Make sure there is agreement on it (you may need to get creative here)
- ➢ Use pictures if children are too young to read
- ➢ Make it colorful

Examples of simple Family Mission Statements:

1. We are patient with each other, and we have fun at home
2. We tell the truth all the time
3. We are cheerful and speak kindly
4. We live a life of healthy choices, good food, we recycle and exercise every day
5. We love each other and give something back to the world every day

6. We find happiness within ourselves and find reasons to praise and support each other
7. We celebrate something – or someone – every day
8. We spend meaningful times together, whether in fun or just in peaceful companionship
9. We don't raise our voices at each other
10. We say sorry if we have hurt someone
11. We pray before each meal, as we are grateful for our food.

When you arrive at an agreement, decide on a symbol or a way of visually reminding family members of your Family Mission Statement. Have the family decide where to put the Family Mission Statement, and when you do, stick the statement where everyone can see it.

Hint:

The more places you post it to, the more effective it will be. You can paste a copy on the fridge, the bathroom mirror, the children's bedroom doors, beside the computer and on bookshelves, at the front door when you come into the house. You can even laminate some and put them on the coffee table, or use as a placemat! This is fun and you can be as creative as your imagination will let you be. Believe me, it is not something your children will ever forget.

Chapter 2: Effective Parenting – A Picture is Worth More Than Words

"Don't worry that children never listen to you; worry that they are always watching you."
- Robert Fulghum

"Children are educated by what the grown-up is and not by his talk."
- Carl Jung

Consider how many times we have said to our child, "Do as I say!" They *hear* you, oh yes! Do you really expect them to do as you say, when your every action, behavior or body language message is shouting the opposite of your words? They *see* you, oh yes!

You need to ask yourself if they are more likely to obey your words or your behaviors.

As the head or co-head of the family, you set the tone for all your family members. Who you are, what you say (and how you say it), and how you behave determines how each day will unfold!

A friend and father (F&F) once asked me (LH) this:

F&F "My son and daughter are just into their teens and I'm seeing a sudden change in their attitudes. They fight all the time and their fights are not minor incidents that you can brush off with a kind word or a stern stare. They get really worked up. Sometimes, they even get physical. These days when I look at them, it's hard for me to believe that here is the little girl who used to carry a pack of gum home just so she could share it with her brother, or here is the young boy who would teach his sister how to throw a baseball. My wife is stressed out and frankly speaking, so am I. I think we're losing it and it really scares me!"

LH "Tell me one thing, Jim. What are your expectations when you get home? What do you feel just before you open the door?"

F&F "It's funny you should ask me that. See, these days I feel just a little afraid before I open the door. Sometimes, when I come in, my kids will be sitting in stony silence or my wife will be very upset, or a struggle of some sort would be underway. Just before I open the door, I take a deep breath and I wonder which one it's going to be today."

LH "So, even before you've entered the house, you have created the reality in your mind. You have envisioned how things are going to be, and you have probably decided on your course of action. Don't you think that is in itself a part of the problem?"

F&F "How can that be? I'm just preparing myself to face the upsets of the evening."

LH "And when you get home that way, what happens? Do you find that there really is something to be upset about?"

F&F "Oh, there almost always is. I just swing into action like a soldier goes into battle. I raise my voice at my children because they won't listen anyway. I'm not proud of it, but I just don't seem to be getting through. I make the kids shush up so

I can have some peace of mind. They sulk and go to their rooms. Believe me, I'm not happy, but at least there's no fighting."

LH "Jim, this evening, why don't you go home with the expectation that things will be OK? And if they are not, think of how you can get your children to cooperate. *Try and conduct yourself the way you want your children to behave.* See if that changes anything. Walk through the door with a smile on your face, and give your wife and children a hug and tell them you missed them."

A week later, Jim thanked me with shining eyes.

F&F "You know what, Lorna, I think it is working. I feel like I'm finally doing something constructive. I feel like I'm leading the way. *I tell myself to take it slowly, to look for the good.* It is interesting as since I've made this change, I can feel that my kids are unsure about my reactions. I've decided that I'll listen to what they have to say and we'll take it from there. My wife does the same now. The fights are still there, but they have reduced and slowly the children have started settling their issues without bringing them to us. Thanks Lorna, I'd never have thought that something so small could really make such a big difference!"

Leadership Versus Management

There is a concept that is highly valued in corporate circles, and it is the essential difference between management and leadership.

Management and leadership are not the same things. While managers do deal with day-to-day issues, pressing details and immediate strategies for current problems, leadership is more about overall purpose, longer-term goals, and direction. It is about seeing where the company wants to be in the future. In successful companies, different sets of people do handle these two types of issues. As parents and CEOs of the family we are running, we do not have that luxury. It is thus only natural that we are more into managing daily squabbles and keeping ourselves above 'water' These tasks can become easier once the course has been set by providing effective leadership, for the long-term success of the family.

The father in the episode related above was over-reactive to the infighting between his children. Of course, constant fights had pulled him into the morass of daily battles and he felt he had no choice but to manage affairs on a daily basis. In doing so, he had lost sight of his ability to lead – to decide with his family what he and they wanted in the long-term.

Are you the kind of parent who feels a clenching in your stomach when your children do something you don't like? Do you rush to the scene of action and pull them apart or put your foot down? Do you prepare for battle with your child and use your bigger size, strength and age to your (unfair) advantage?

If you do, you may come off feeling that things have been sorted out and stability has been restored. But the normalcy you've just established is a myth. Guess what happens when you turn your back, or step out of the room?

For all outward appearances, your children may have submitted, but they are boiling inside. The edifice of your victory over your children is standing on the remains of a shattered relationship. You have just fallen short of your own teachings ('don't fight', 'isn't there a better way to solve your problems?', 'why can't you settle differences in a friendly manner?') Your children go away from the situation with suppressed emotions that could come out in uglier ways when you least expect it.

I remember once when Carly was just four years old, she had some soft dolls, and a teddy bear that a favorite aunt had given her. Those dolls were exceptionally beautiful and extremely cuddly. To my daughter of course, her dolls were prized possessions, so, when her birthday party came around, she naturally wanted to show them off in front of her friends. In spite of fair warning from me, she brought out four of her cuddly dolls and put them up for display. Then, she refused to allow a single child in the room to touch any of them.

The children were obviously curious. They wanted to touch, cuddle and squeeze. Carly was horrified at the sight of all those hands coming at her dolls from all directions. I could feel the change in the atmosphere as a silent war of little wills raged on. Soon, our lovely little party was beginning to get dangerously close to a skirmish. In an effort to make things right, I spoke to Carly in my brightest voice and my best 'mama bear' smile "Sweetie, please share the dolls with your friends". I did not get anything from Carly, except a stubborn stare and two little arms that hugged the dolls a little tighter. My tone faltered a bit and I tried again, this time in my strict 'do it or else' voice. My little daughter just stood there and shouted, "No, I'm not sharing". The sudden silence in the room embarrassed me. I could feel myself reddening, while 10 pairs of curious eyes switched from me to Carly and back.

Later that night, when I went to kiss my daughter goodnight, I saw that she was already asleep. She was holding four dolls in her arms and clutching them tight even in her sleep. I gently tried to draw the toys away, but even in her sleep, Carly refused to let go!

It took me – a mother with 2 older boys – some time to understand that some children behave in a particular way due to various reasons. My sons never had a problem sharing anything and everything. My daughter was the opposite. I could not figure that out. So? I interpreted her resistance as an affront.

It was foolish of me to expect uninhibited sharing from a child so young. Carly was too young to understand why she had to share. I needed to show her the direction and guide her gently into the spirit of sharing. As a parent, that was my role. In that situation, I decided to 'manage' things. I let my emotions get in the way and forgot that I was coming across as a wrong role model to my daughter. My words were asking her to share, but my actions were showing her that I could pluck away her things if and when I wanted to. Do you see how my actions were getting in the way of the values I wanted to teach my little girl? Do you see how I became a reactive parent, instead of a proactive parent?

> Lead the way, your children will follow.

The best way to get your children to do something is to do it yourself first. Show them what your expectations are, by living your expectations.

If you do not want fighting and verbal abuse in your homes, *restrain yourself first*. Do not use foul and abusive language. Not ever. Not when driving (a challenge sometimes). Not over the phone. Treat your partner/spouse and friends with respect and use courteous words with everyone, whether it is the youngest member of the family, the florist, a passing person you meet on the street, the bus driver, or the grocery clerk.

I remember hearing this interesting story from a parent. Her son was asked to bring a blanket to school for the annual picnic. As asked, the boy took a blanket to school on the appointed day *without asking his mother*. When he came home, he saw his mother frantically looking at the blanket hanging out of his knapsack. The blanket was now spotted with stains. Horrified, she asked him where he had taken the blanket and why he had not asked permission. She was really not happy that he had not asked her permission first. Tearfully, the little boy answered. "But Mom, you know Dad never asks his boss for permission before he brings home the computer paper from his office!"

➢ If you want your children to become good individuals, walk YOUR talk.

Be the person of high integrity that you want your children to be. We are the yardsticks with which our children measure the realities around them. "If it's okay for dad to go to the office late, it's okay for me to be late!"

Never tell your children a lie for they are sure to catch you at it. It doesn't matter if it is a white, green, purple or black lie. What matters is that you are teaching the wrong values.

One day I had gone to visit one of my closest friends, Sue. As I sat there at her kitchen table, watching her send off her kids one by one to school, I felt – more than saw – the love and care she was taking with each one of them.

When her youngest boy Stevie came to say goodbye, he asked his mom, "Mom, what should I tell the teacher? Shall I just tell her that I was sick and did not get my homework done?"
"No, Stevie", Sue shot back immediately. "Don't lie, ever. Tell your teacher the truth: that you forgot to do it. Ask if you could do double

homework tonight to make up for it. I think your teacher will understand."

"But mom, what will she think if I say that?" Stevie countered in all innocence.

Susan hugged him saying, "I think she will appreciate that you are willing to tell the truth. Always tell the truth."

That conversation has stayed with me to this day. When I'm tempted to cook up a quick excuse, those words stop me. Sue is an excellent mother that has raised three wonderful children. She set the standard very early as a parent, and lived by the rule herself.

Have you ever noticed how some children are naturally well mannered, soft-spoken and pleasant in their interactions with others? You may also have come across children who are boisterous, disruptive, callous and downright rude. I knew a mother who was always complaining of her little girl's tendency to argue. Little did the mother realize that she had herself implanted this behavior in her child. Teach your children to be courteous and gentle. Use 'Please', and 'Thank you' liberally in your language. This will persuade your children to do the same.

Teach your children to greet others in a warm and sincere manner. Teach them to look another person in the eye, teach them how to shake hands and say, "Nice to meet you". Show them how they can be gracious. Ask them to hold doors open for others, but before you do that, follow these practices yourself.

Are you the person you want your child to be? Everything you do, and don't do, sends silent messages to your children. Make sure that your messages convey the values you want to pass on.

Becoming a good role model is not very easy. However, it is not difficult either if you prepare yourself in a certain way.

- ➢ Understand who you are. Take the time to evaluate your values. Once you have done so, be consistent with what you insist on.
- ➢ Face your own demons before you set out to pass on your belief systems to others. Parents who most often see the glass as half empty instead of half full, can easily transfer defeating beliefs to their children.
- ➢ Take responsibility for your actions. If you do something wrong, accept it and own it. If you slip up in front of your children, admit it, ask for forgiveness, and accept your faults graciously. This will teach them how to accept their mistakes.
- ➢ Nurture the qualities you wish to pass on. Enjoy, exercise, laugh, eat healthy and be compassionate.
- ➢ Practice spirituality and explain your spiritual beliefs to your children.
- ➢ When we understand who we are, and take care of who we want to become, we provide our children with the kind of positive role models they need.

Exercise:

Take some time alone, and figure out the values that you want to pass on. Remember that 'values' include beliefs (spiritual or other), ethics or the moral code you adhere to, standards that you set for yourself, rules that you follow, and the like.

Then write them down, like so:

- ✓ I will be honest and truthful in my deeds and words. I will not lie in front of my children. For me, honesty is not a matter of convenience. I will honor my word with my children and with everyone else. I realize that my children are learning the values of honesty and integrity from me.

- ✓ I will show respect to everyone around me, no matter what they look like or where they are from. This respect includes my children and our pets. I will use the kind of language that I want my children to use. I will exercise self-restraint and expect the same discipline from myself that I exercise on my children. I will not make excuses or shift blame. I understand that my children are learning values of respect and responsibility from me.

- ✓ I will treat my children equally and will make proper use of the power I have. I will not take criticism to heart and will judge others based on facts. I understand that my children are learning values of fair dealings from me.

- ✓ I will make and eat healthy food. I will eat regularly and on time. I will choose nutritious snacks, watch portion sizes, exercise and maintain my proper weight. I will not eat while watching TV, talking on the phone or working on the computer. I understand that my children are learning values of good eating from me.

- ✓ I will obey laws, perform my civic duties, avoid littering, recycle, and do my best to prevent pollution. I understand that my children are learning values of a good citizen from me.

- ✓ I will focus on the positive. I will avoid being negative and criticizing myself or others. I will spread positive thoughts and positive energy all around me. I understand that my children are learning values of positive thinking from me.

Chapter 3: Disciplining with Creativity

"Children should have enough freedom to be themselves – once they've learned the rules."
- Anna Quindlen

"My mother protected me from the world and my father threatened me with it."
- Quentin Crisp

Too often, we label our friends who are parents according to their disciplinary style ... or apparent lack thereof. Maybe we also label our parenting partner in a similar way. We may say, "He holds the stick" or "She is a real softie."

The truth is that there are a number of parenting styles, and not all of them have to do with how we discipline our children.

When we remember what the best school teachers say – that there are no bad or unteachable students, only teachers who can't figure out how to reach them – we must agree to say the same thing about parents!

A mother once related a touching story about her little boy.

> She was pregnant at that time and her son had observed his father doing the dinner dishes while she took a much-needed rest. One afternoon, the mother served the little boy his lunch and went up to her room to rest. When she came back downstairs after an hour, she was shocked by the sight that greeted her. Her son had dragged a low stool to the sink and he had washed the dishes she had left there from lunch. The

mother also saw that the young boy had made a mess with water splashed over the counter, dripping on the floor and had completely soaked the front of his shirt and sleeves. The mother's first impulse was to express unhappiness with his initiative. The expectant look in her son's eyes stopped her short. She asked him what he was doing. He explained that he wanted to help her with the dishes, just as his father did.

"Well, what about all this water, Billy?" she asked gently. "Don't you think we should do something about it?"

The little boy thought for a second and ran to fetch the mop. Then he made his mommy sit near the counter while he wiped the water off. "The sight touched my heart. I could not believe that my small boy was trying to put on his papa's shoes to help me. Being upset with the excess water that day would have crushed his helping spirit. I had to do some extra work after he had finished, but that was alright considering that my boy was learning to help around the house."

An important lesson in discipline waits for us in all situations. You will understand what it is as you read on. Before that, let us understand what discipline really is.

Children create many challenging situations for their parents. Sometimes, we are amused, but most of the times, we feel frustrated, guilty or embarrassed. Often, your child is your alter ego. How he or she behaves and acts is sometimes seen as a measure of your own worthiness.

Every parent wants the perfect child. We compare, urge, complain and punish, all in our pursuit of perfection. We want well-adjusted, well-balanced, well-behaved, well-mannered, well-this and well-that children.

However, what we *want* is sometimes very different from what we have. Repeating instructions until we are ready to keel over, arguing, nagging, manipulating, threatening and quarrelling – all in a day's work! Even then, we are unable to get our children to do what we want, just the way <u>we</u> want it!

Little children are like little saplings sprouting in the forest. These saplings are young and tender. They need enough water and nutrients to grow. However, unless they are pruned and trimmed, they will shoot out new branches in uneven angles and become ugly and unkempt. Their growth will slowly come to an end and they will start yellowing and drooping. Trimming ensures that plants become healthy, thick and vibrant. Discipline does the same for children.

Why Do Children Misbehave?

All children misbehave. In reality, they only think they are testing their power, their boundaries and their wings.

All responsible parents discipline or correct their children as best as they can. Whether their disciplinary methods are right or effective is a matter that we will look into a little later. Before you can make up your mind about what method you adopt, you have to understand why your child is misbehaving.

- → Attention. Sometimes, children just want immediate attention. When children 'act up' to get your attention, ignore their misbehavior, unless they are hurting themselves, someone else or damaging property. If you are busy at the time, which is usually the case, let them know when you will spend time with them, for example, when you return from work, get off the phone, or stop looking at the computer etc.

- Unwell. Very young children misbehave when they are sick, tired or hungry. As a parent, it is up to you to schedule your activities in such a way as to take care of the interests of your child.

- Test. As children grow, they are reinventing themselves; they are also reinventing you and their relationship with you. Sometimes, they just want to test you because they want to know whether you really mean what you say. That is why it is important to hang on to your decision. Parents who waver and give in to their children's tantrums are indirectly sending the wrong messages. They are telling their children that if they cry and whine hard enough, they will finally get their way.

- Guilt. Sometimes children misbehave because they feel bad about themselves. They feel bad about something they have done or said, therefore, they act badly. When this happens, encourage your child to look at the positive side of things. Give them something to be happy about.

- Freedom. Teenagers often misbehave because they are growing up and they yearn to be independent. They want to make their own decisions, so they demand more freedom. However, their decisions may not always be the best decisions. You will find your horns locked over many things, from growing long hair to wearing torn jeans, getting a tattoo or piercing. When this happens, take a break. Cool off. But do not allow your differences to come between you. Do not freeze out your teenager. Keep the channels of communication open. Remember, as children grow they no longer accept your choices as being automatically correct.

- Confusion. Quite often, children misbehave because they do not know what is expected of them or they forget what they are supposed to do. Make your expectations clear by expressing your limits in terms of what they should and should not do. Set age-appropriate limits.

Disciplining children is hard work and many parents fail in their job. Not because they lack love ... and definitely not because they don't want what is best for their children. Many parents fail because they are inconsistent. They say one thing and mean quite another. They threaten but do not follow through. They punish in anger, without taking the time to understand. The biggest hurdle in the path of a child's discipline training can be the parent. I'm sorry to say this; however, it's true.

There is an old story of a young man sentenced to life imprisonment after he was found guilty of a heinous crime.

> While passing his judgment, the King wanted to know whether the young man had anything to say.
>
> "Yes, your Majesty", the young man replied. "Please punish my parents to 10 years of rigorous imprisonment. Every day, when I look out of my prison, I want to see them toiling away."
>
> The King was surprised. "Why?" he asked. "Do you dislike your parents so much?"
>
> The young man replied, "Your Majesty, when I was a young boy, I used to steal pencils, erasers and books. My parents encouraged me to bring home more stolen goods so they did not have to spend money. So, when I grew up, I started stealing bigger things. They have made me what I am. Do you think it is fair that I suffer the fruits of their labor alone?"

While this is just a story with a strong moral, you can see the kernel of truth shining through. Your children are like raw dough or soft clay. You can mold them into whatever you wish. If, in the end you find yourself saying, "I tried my best, but he never was a good child", you should understand that half the responsibility of what your child has become lies squarely on your shoulders.

When it comes to discipline and making corrections, every parent has their own ideas of right and wrong. Some believe that children ought to make their own decisions from the very beginning. Others do not trust their grown children to take any decision. Some rule with the rod, others feel that their children will grow up nicely if they just leave them alone. Suffice to say that there is no single, right way to go about it. Also, whatever you do, some amount of misbehavior is normal. However, knowing how to react to misbehavior is important.

> **Strange Fact**: Normally, children do not misbehave just to make their parents miserable. In fact, children delight in pleasing their parents. They have a natural tendency to please and look for approval in all that they do.

Parents who make use of this principle in their strategies for discipline reap quick and everlasting results. When parents approve positive behavior, they are reinforcing the desired behavior. This, I believe, is the best way to discipline your child if you want lasting results. There is one universal principle underlying *successful* discipline tactics: ***Discipline children so they will want to behave.***

Sounds a little cryptic, doesn't it? Let me explain.

Effective discipline is 'loving discipline'. This sort of discipline is based on a healthy relationship with your child. To discipline your child effectively, you must first know your child. Take the time to understand what makes them happy or sad. Find out which buttons excite, please and provoke them. Connect with your child early, and be positive.

Every child is unique in his or her way. (Even identical twins have their own unique traits – they are not identical at all, you may find). Never judge one child by the behaviors or achievements of another. Study your child and understand his or her capabilities at various ages. Your expectations from your child should match these capabilities. It is interesting to me that a parent will giggle over their child's bad behavior and think it cute. The child has an uncanny way of knowing the response they have evoked. It becomes very difficult for the parent to discipline, and confusing to the child, when something is funny one day, and causes anger to the parent the next day.

Think like your child. Little adults think and behave in ways that may seem crazy to us. When a young child rolls in a puddle, they don't want to get sick or ruin their clothing. They are perhaps only looking for the pleasure of cool water on a warm body, or to see how high a splash will go. For most children, impulse dictates behavior and impulses demand instant gratification. They do not misbehave to defy, instead they act upon their impulses – in order to test their power, spread their wings and experience the world.

Successful parents with well-behaved children usually have a game plan. They have short-term goals and they also work towards larger goals. They connect good behavior with feelings of achievement. For them, good behavior is a cause for celebration.

Successful parents evoke respect, not fear in their children. A loving parent has to be both warm and wise. When your baby is very young, you nurture him or her with love. As they grow older, you gently guide them into the behavioral patterns you believe are right. Here, you must understand the difference between being in charge and being in control. You cannot control your child's behavior. You can only carry out your responsibilities in such a way as to make the child understand who is in charge. Children respond favorably to genuine trust and respect.

Successful parents anticipate issues in advance of them occurring. They are prepared for the worst, and yet hope for the best. They know how to handle tantrums, arguments, power struggles, disobedience and fighting.

Successful parents are proactive. They are strict but positive. They discipline and correct, but do not keep their love under wraps. They understand change and are open to it. Most importantly, they delight in their children and do not allow misbehavior to come in the way of their enjoyment of their children.

Of course, part of the problem is that some parents do not know whether they are parenting their children in an effective and desirable manner. Sometimes things work out well, and other times they question their skills.

Parenting Styles

We pick up most of our parenting styles from our parents.

When I was a teenager, I remember thinking that I would never raise my voice at my children. I had seen this happen around me, and I knew it was not something I liked. This became an important focus of my parenting consciousness. At times, it was a strain to not to break this promise to myself, however I remembered how much it scared me as a child, when I heard adults raising their voices.

We most often discipline as we were disciplined.

We also talk, discuss, learn and mimic our parents. Even so, much of what we do is based on guesswork. We do our best and hope that we're doing the right thing. Using all the information we have, we adopt a style of parenting that we feel is best suited for our children.

What makes it more interesting and complex, is that when there are two parents raising a child, chances are that there will be differences in the styles of the parents. These parenting styles can be broadly divided into:

1. **Indulgent:** This parenting style is more sensitive to their child's needs than they are strict. They do not lay down too many rules, and even the few rules they insist upon can be wriggled out of, bent or altered. Children of such a parenting style may have high levels of imagination, creativity and self-esteem; but can lack motivation. They may end up being poor achievers, as they may find it difficult to conform to the rules of society.

2. **Authoritarian:** This parenting style is at the other extreme of the parent style. This parent can be very strict and often considered insensitive. Their rules are unbending, clearly laid out and inviolable. Children of such a parent may have high motivation and could do well in school. On the other hand, they may suffer low self-esteem and self-confidence. Children disciplined by an Authoritarian parent may have poor social skills and could suffer from depression.

3. **Uninvolved:** This parenting style is not demanding and often shows very low levels of responsiveness to the child. Children of such a parent can be low in self-esteem and low in motivation. In extreme cases, children raised by this parenting style can be neglectful and uncaring. This is not just about latchkey kids; children who don't benefit from communication with a parent who is home are in the same boat.

4. **Assertive:** This parenting style is demanding and responsive towards the child. They have clear standards and rules that children are expected to follow. At the same time, they are not intrusive or restrictive. They are supportive, not punitive,

in their disciplinary methods. They set limits and expect their children to respect these limits. They want their children to become socially responsible, motivated and cooperative.

Here is a diagrammatic representation of the categories parents fall into to give you a quick idea:

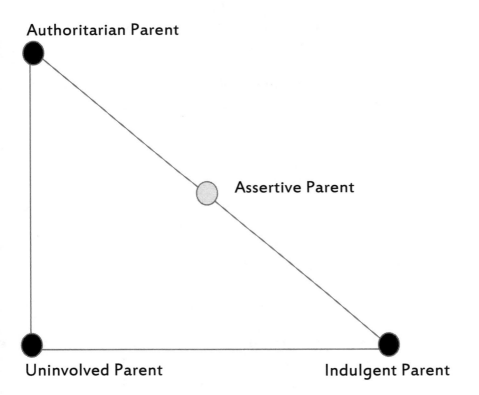

PARENTING STYLES

What kind of parent are you? Take the quiz at the end of this chapter to find out.

Ways to Discipline or Change Behavior Effectively

Successful parents make discipline or changing behavior fun. Yes, that's correct – FUN. They experiment, talk, ask, listen and answer. There are fun and creative ways to discipline your child, so you get the point across without causing hurt and bad feelings. Of course as a parent, you know when this is the best approach for the situation you are facing. Certainly, there are times when thresholds have been crossed, that fun is not the object to 'learning a lesson'.

One father shared this story with me.

> "Our little boy William suddenly started leaving the seat of the toilet up. Often, he would forget to flush the toilet. This was distressing and strange. Short of reminding him and checking on him every time, there seemed to be no way out. Since we entertained a lot, my wife was always afraid of William leaving the toilet soiled and the seat up.
>
> Then one day, my wife spoke to him about the importance of keeping the toilets clean. She told him that she was concerned that some of the little guests who came home would dirty the toilets and forget to clean up after themselves. William came up with a bright solution for the problem. He said that we should put up signs reminding people to clean up after they used the toilets. That's exactly what we did. We put up colorful little picture cards with the necessary instructions on the inside of the bathroom door. Ostensibly, this was for our guests, but the cards had their

desired effect on William, too. After that, we never had to check up on our son again. Since he had helped make the picture cards, it became a matter of priority for him too."

Boundaries Help

Children need the reassurance of boundaries. Limits provide a safe structure within which children can operate. They may test these limits from time to time, but believe me, they are reassured by the presence of these limits. Expect your children to obey your rules. Your children will rise to your expectations, consciously or unconsciously.

One of the most effective ways of disciplining your child is to be very clear about the ground rules. Set limits and explain to your child what they can and cannot do in definite terms.

In our home, we have definite rules about important things, like getting home before 11 on weekends, calling or texting to say where you are, taking money from my wallet only after asking, staying over at a friend's house, and internet browsing guidelines. We have arrived at most of these rules through consensus and all my children know the things that concern me. To remind them of these rules, at one point I posted them on the refrigerator with my children's signature on it. My children know that breaking these rules will have consequences.

When Carly wants to talk on the phone past 10:00 pm, we have an already established rule, which is, she gets off the phone at 9:30 the following night to compensate for the time. She is not allowed to use the computer in her bedroom; she must use it in the family room. The best part is that since we already have established the rules, there was no need for upset as we have discussed this in advance.

My point is, there are constructive ways in which you can discipline your child. The old proverb, "Spare the rod and spoil your child" does not hold water. Reprimanding your child should be your last resort — and never, ever in public. Spanking, I would say, should be a strict 'no-no'. Disciplining your child through fear, pain or control policies will only teach them to hide, lie and run away. Being overly lenient will make them flippant and uncaring. When it comes to discipline, you cannot always go by your heart alone. While love, affection and warmth are essential, you also have to grow a heart of steel, and be as creative as possible.

There is a delicate balance between good and bad behavior. This balance keeps changing over time. As parents, we have to be there to monitor the changing behavioral patterns of our children, supporting them when they need encouragement and reproving them gently, yet effectively, when they step out of line.

Disciplining through Reprimand

To most of us, reprimanding wrong behavior is a big part of disciplining. Have you ever noticed how we reprimand our children? We usually start off by expressing our disapproval. "Well, Danielle, you did it again, didn't you? How could you do this? I just don't know what to tell your dad. He is going to be so disappointed in you." And how do we offer praise? "Wow, that's great. What a smart girl you are. Daddy's going to be so proud of you."

Did you notice that we are offering <u>*conditional*</u> appreciation and disapproval here? "Do something nice and we will be proud of you; do something undesirable and we will be miserable *because of you*!" Is there another way of saying this? "You had better behave or else!"

Do you see why so much of our 'pressure parenting' ricochets off the heads of children? Nobody likes to be offered conditional love, most of all children.

Discipline your children so they feel bad about their behavior and *not about themselves.*

To understand the above, ask yourself this: How do you feel when someone criticizes your behavior? You get <u>defensive</u>, right? Don't you think the same applies to your child? Now, let us change the scenario a little.

> Suppose you are late getting into your office. Your boss calls you the moment you arrive. You know you're about to get told off and you feel rotten inside. When you get there, your boss asks you to sit down. You can see that he is not pleased.
>
> He speaks politely but firmly, "Phil, I know you have told me about issues at home. Looking after twins and taking care of your pregnant wife is a tough order. I'm impressed that you are getting here in the first place. But Phil, we have a business to run. I can't have you coming late to the office. You're the manager here. Can you imagine what example you're setting for those who work for you? Don't you think it is unfair to demand punctuality from others when you can't follow through yourself? You're a good employee, one of our best and I really like you. Please do whatever you have to and come to the office on time. I expect you to follow through, Phil."

Whoosh! With a dressing down like that, chances are, if he wants to keep his job, Phil is not going to be late again.

Now, this strategy works wonders even when it comes to reprimanding your children.

In the first part of the reprimand, the boss expresses his *sympathy* with what Phil is going through. As a parent, there is a wealth of strategy here. Whenever your kids step out of line, start off by stating the misdemeanor and expressing your understanding or sympathy. Make them feel that you understand a part of their problem. "Dan, you spoke rudely to your mom. I can understand that you were angry about misplacing your keys."

From there, go on to express the feelings your child's misbehavior has evoked in you. "I am upset", "I am sad", "I am very angry at this behavior", "what you have just done makes me so sad" and so forth. This expresses your *disapproval of the behavior*.

The next part is where the core of the strategy lies: You show your child that <u>you love *him*</u> and that it is his behavior that has upset you. "I love you. I just don't think that this is the right way to behave" or 'Your acting up tonight at the dinner table was painful, but you are a good person. You're better than that kind of behavior."

Allow your child to feel your sadness, anger, disappointment or disapproval. *However, let him know that these feelings are directed at the action, not at them.* This makes all the difference.

And then, discuss with it your child so they understand that every action brings a consequence with it. Consequences are learning experiences. They are hard for the parent but necessary for the child.

Once you're done with the scolding, let it go completely. Do not carry it in your heart for the rest of the day or week. Do not rehash it with your child. Snide remarks and hurtful comments can break your child's spirit, even more than a spanking! When you spank a child, you change who they are, so never, ever, spank your child.

A mother I knew who was quite a sensitive woman came to me one day with tears in her eyes.

"Lorna", she said, "you've got to help me. Recently, my daughter has started showing a preference for her dad. While I'm happy for her dad, I feel scared that I'm losing my little girl. When I try to read to her, she starts crying. If I ask her to do something, she acts as if she hasn't heard. It's like she is blocking me out. But when it's her dad asking her to do those things, she is so eager to please. I don't understand it!"

After a little talking, we got to the crux of her problem. This mother carried the pain and grudge of her daughter's misdemeanor in her heart and *made snide remarks about past misbehavior whenever she could*. For instance, if her daughter had spilt her milk two days back, this mother would carry on about it for at least a week, and link all future misdemeanors with the spilling of the milk. "You are careless. See, you've lost your book today. Just like you dropped you milk last week" or "Why can't you do anything right? Is that the way you draw that picture? You're not getting good grades because you're impatient. No wonder you spilt your milk last week and lost your book yesterday."

Do you see the pattern here?

Do you remember to acknowledge any changes in behaviour? If you see your child has made their bed, after scolding them for not making their bed, and they do so for a few days in a row, do you remember to encourage them and take the time to acknowledge the new behaviour?

Rules to Follow While Reprimanding Unacceptable Behavior

- Reprimand *immediately*, if possible, time in-between the action and the consequence is confusing to a child.

- Be firm. Do not allow yourself to get distracted from the important business of expressing your disapproval and looking for a solution.

- Look your child straight in the eye when you scold them.

- Express your dissatisfaction and your sadness about their actions.

- Express your expectations so your child knows what they were supposed to do.

- Be consistent. You cannot waver in what is acceptable and what is not. If it is unacceptable once, it is unacceptable always!

- Once you finish with the scolding, make sure to let your anger go. Like us, children also do not like to be reminded of their misdeeds and follies.

- Never vent your anger by calling names or getting physically abusive. Go for a walk, leave the room and deal with your emotions.

- Give your child a chance to express what he or she is feeling. If your child takes you up on your offer, listen to him attentively and wholeheartedly. Maybe there is a point in what he or she is saying that you did not see before.

➤ After the episode, touch your child in a way that expresses your love. Connect with him in some way so they feel that you still love and accept him, even while you reject his behavior.

Reprimanding is not the only way of disciplining your child. In fact, I think it must be the last way. There are other ways to mold your child's behavior.

Why Discipline Your Child?

Disciplining your child takes time, effort and will. It is not an easy or quick process. You have to be at it consistently before you start seeing the results you want. Let me assure you, it is worth every bit of the effort you put in.

Mistakes

Given below are some of the mistakes parents often make, sometimes out of ignorance, misplaced goodwill or downright laziness. These mistakes, recurring over a period of time, will only lead your child into sloppiness and delinquency:

- Giving a child everything they want will make them believe that the world owes them everything. They will never get into the mood to earn what they want.

- Never laugh with your child or give way to amusement when your child uses bad language. If they think that using unacceptably language will give them attention, they are likely to repeat this behavior.

- Never pick up the things that they leave lying around. Ask them to do these themselves so that they grow up to be responsible. If they don't pick up after themselves, perhaps those things should be put away out of their reach for a bit, so they may appreciate the consequences of their actions.

- Just as you are careful with what goes into their bodies, keep a close watch on what goes into their minds. Let their mind not feed on garbage. Be mindful of the TV they watch, songs they listen to, websites they visit, etc.

- Teach your child to respect and value money. Never give them the outrageous amount they may ask for, even if it is within your means. Monitor how they spend money and encourage them to buy their own gifts. Go to www.thewealthyteen.com to review information on "The Wealthy Teen" which discusses how parents and mentors can assist teens and pre-teens with money issues.

- Give your child strong ethical and moral values – shared by all in your family – so that they have something to fall back on during the difficult times of their lives.

- If your child is wrong, tell them so. Hiding it from them will only condition them to believe that the world is against them.

One of the two essential qualities that a parent should have is *patience*.

Even when you know that you are giving all you've got and that you're trudging the right path, results may be slow in coming. Some children test you longer than others. Accept it as part of their charm! Maybe you have one child that needs more support; you have to hold their hand a little longer than their sibling.

This is where the second most important quality will help, *faith*. Have patience and faith. Together, they will see you through.

Quiz

Take this quiz and find out what kind of a parent you are.

Answer pattern:

1: Always   2: Rarely   3: Never

The number given in brackets is the score for the corresponding choice.

1	You have to constantly remind your child when you want them to do something. 1(0) 2(2) 3(5)
2	Your child plays rough with other children and you let them get away with it. 1(0) 2(2) 3(4)
3	When your children fight, you yell at them and send them to their rooms. 1(6) 2(3) 3(0)
4	Your children follow set schedules as to when they are expected home at night. 1(4) 2(1) 3(0)
5	Your child cleans personal space after playing, studying, drawing or eating. 1(4) 2(1) 3(0)

6	When your child misbehaves, they know there will be a reckoning when you find out. 1(6) 2(2) 3(0)
7	Your children throw tantrums when they want something and will whine until he gets it. 1(0) 2(1) 3(4)
8	Your children have fixed chores around the house that they are expected to carry out WITHOUT promptings. 1(4) 2(1) 3(0)
9	Your constant nagging tires you out by the end of the day. 1(4) 2(1) 3(0)
10	Your child indulges in some harmless 'name calling' and you act as if you've not heard. 1(0) 2(1) 3(4)
11	You spank your child. 1(6) 2(1) 3(0)
12	You make all the rules in the house and expect them to be followed implicitly. 1(6) 2(2) 3(0)

Scores:

15 – 20:	You may be an indulgent parent.
<14:	You may be an uninvolved parent
20- 30:	You may be an assertive parent
>30:	You may be an authoritarian parent.

This quiz will help you identify your style of parenting. You can then make changes in your style to become the kind of parent you desire to be. Changing your style may seem to be a little difficult. Sometimes, disciplining your child consistently and effectively may, in itself, seem like a big task. Nonetheless discipline is important because this is what makes your child the best they can be, instead of the individual they just happened to be.

Chapter 4: Connecting with Love

"Children learn to smile from their parents."
- Shinichi Suzuki

*"I don't think my parents liked me.
They put a live teddy bear in my crib."*
- Woody Allen

The only thing any of us – at whatever age – want is love. Our worst behaviors are driven by that search for love that we don't believe we have. Our biggest sense of inferiority or failure comes from the erroneous belief that we are not lovable. We are all dying inside to hear the words, "You are lovable; I love you; you are loved."

You don't really have to be a child psychologist to know what your child needs the most from you: undivided love, focused attention and TLC – tender loving care.

I am sure every parent knows and understands this in their hearts and we feel that we are doing just that – bringing up our children with all the love and care that they need.

However, there is often a gap between what you feel as a parent and what you express to your child.

If you don't agree with me, answer the following questions:

- → Do you demonstrate your love physically? Do you appropriately hug, touch, pat, kiss and cuddle your child?

- When your child speaks to you, do you look into their eyes and listen to them wholeheartedly, or do you 'hmmmm' and 'ohhhhh' your way through a predominantly one-sided conversation ... with your back turned away?

- Do you encourage your children to talk about their school, teachers, friends and their dreams?

- Do you greet your children when they get home, or do your kids walk in and out of your life without so much as a 'hello'?

- When was the last time you played with your child and had fun doing it?

- Do you watch television together?

- Do you eat together?

- Do you spend one-on-one time with each of your children?

- When your child asks you a question, do you take the time to explain things or do you brush it off saying 'you're not old enough to understand'? Do you look them in the eyes when you respond?

- Do you discuss your financial situation (as appropriate), constraints and concerns with your children?

- Do you make it a point to do fun activities together?

- As age appropriate, do you share your life lessons with them?

How many of the above questions did you answer in the negative? The count should give you some indication of the gap between the feelings within you and their actual manifestation.

I do not mean to point accusing fingers at anyone. As parents, we do the best we can with whatever time we have at our disposal. Each one of us knows that there is room for improvement but when life presses on you with other demands, you may lose focus. You lose sight of your most important duties, simply because there is no one to remind you of them. There are no deadlines, no angry boss to pacify and no check waiting to be cashed if the job is done well. It is human nature to focus on what is urgent and pressing. So quite naturally, we may lose sight of those important matters that do not evoke a sense of urgency. In short, we are programmed to wait until things reach a level of urgency before we take corrective action. It is not in us to build dams unless there is an impending threat of deluge!

Big Parenting Mistake: We often forget the wisdom behind the words, "It is better to be safe than sorry".

Parenting is a tough job, as too often you forge ahead on your own steam, without any guidelines or benchmarks. While all the things we need to do as parents are important, they are not necessarily urgent. A sense of urgency develops only when things have deteriorated.

If we neglect our parenting duties, by design or accident, our relationships begin to deteriorate. The sad part is, we often do not realize what is happening until things are sometimes too far gone, and have started turning ugly. When that happens, we need urgent repair work and artificial bandaging does not work.

Think of a teen that has started to use drugs, and the signs were there for parents. However, they were too busy to notice or deal with them. By the time the police or school have become involved, it is much more of a problem to sort out.

Ironically, if you spend some time every day doing the important things, then the number of urgent issues coming up later – like addiction or violence – will reduce substantially. That is why it is vital to stay connected with your children at all times.

When we take the time and the effort to stay connected, our children already know our expectations. A broad framework of our hopes and principles is in place and even if the children stray a little, they will keep falling back into the invisible limits set by our standards.

Everything that is not consciously attended to, cared for, nurtured and renewed will ultimately atrophy. Your relationship with your children is no exception.

When your child is younger, he or she will be moved by your show of emotion. When it comes to your teens and pre-teens, emotional language will get you nowhere.

As children grow older, too much emotion will only embarrass them. That is why you have to keep your emotional bank account full of cash from the time your children are small. Just as you can repair a broken china pot, a relationship that has ruptured can also be mended. But the crack will always show.

In this chapter, I want to explore ways in which you can keep your family bonded together through constant care and nurture. I believe that this topic is all the more important today when we have social cultures and traditions pulling the family apart.

In the good old days, when we were young, things were a lot different. First of all, TV times were reduced, and there was no Internet, and cell phones and messaging didn't exist. As children, we loved to play games with the children in the neighborhood while our parents chatted. Visiting neighbors and family – taking a walk around the neighborhood as a family – was a time-honored tradition. Also, there were a number of activities that brought the entire community together, like barbeques, overnight camps, summer street parties, and gatherings for sports events. Life was more laid back then.

This is not so true anymore. Many children today come from two-income families, or a one-income family where they live with a parent who is stretched to the maximum (time-wise, emotionally, and maybe financially). When parents are working, there is immense pressure on family time. Most of the time, the focus is on getting things done, not coming together and having fun. It is very difficult to spend quality time with your family when you rush back from the office at 7 p.m. every night through the week. At that point, your priority is to get food on the table, get the children do their homework and then get them washed and in bed, so you can get some rest. Weekends are busier still, with shopping, cleaning cooking and socializing. To put it simply, we just don't have enough time to spend with our children and this, more than anything else, is doing the most harm to our family structures.

One man wrote to me asking for coaching:

> "Dear Lorna, my wife and I need help. We were childhood sweethearts. We were in love for six long years before we got married. After marriage, for a while, we lived as if we were in a dream. Two years later, our son Marc came along. Things changed completely. Bev had to give up her job because we did not have anyone to help out with the baby. She did not like it, but there was no helping it. Two years later, we had Anthony. The unexpected arrival of our second son put us in a tizzy. Most nights, Bev slept in the nursery with the children. When I reached home late at night, I would hardly get to see Bev because she was so busy with the children.
>
> Then, when things started settling down a little, Bev got a new job. It was a marketing job. She had a target and as long as she

met it, she could work flexible hours. So we made an arrangement: Bev would work from late afternoon into the night, while I worked from early morning until evening. That meant our children were with a sitter for only two hours a day.

Things were working out fine for some time. Bev would work from home in the mornings, getting her paperwork done, so she could go straight to client meetings. I would carry my work home so I could leave the office before 5 pm.

But lately, we have all been feeling sad. Somehow, that 'family feeling' (if you know what I mean) is missing. Even when we go out, it seems like we are in our own worlds. Marc has become very shy and insecure. He hardly talks to anyone and likes to play alone. Even if we try to play with him, he ignores us. Anthony is a weepy boy. He cries all the time and sticks to Bev as if he is afraid to let go. This rubs us raw. My wife and I feel that something has gone terribly wrong, but we just don't know what it is. We have become a shadow of what we were, although we are still working very hard. Can you please offer us some advice? "

Seeing the problem from the other side of the table, we all know what has gone wrong. None of them can see the visible marks of love in the form of companionship, sharing or playing. This family has become dysfunctional. The parents are too busy with their work to pay much attention to their children, to each other, or themselves. Their children are suffering from the lack of *tangible* love in the house. They do not understand that their parents are driving themselves up the wall because they want what is best for them. So they quietly fold into their own worlds and stay there, maturing much before their time and carrying love-parched hearts throughout their lives.

The 'family feeling' that the father was talking about is a feeling of comfort together, that feeling of oneness and unity created through interweaving bonds of love, responsibilities, trust and faith. It comes through companionship, shared targets and common dreams. Even disagreements and arguments play a part in this. The 'family feeling' is the sum total of all the things that we do within our family that gives us a sense of belonging, and a sense that we are important to each other.

Children thrive on a healthy and strong family feeling.

It gives them security and shows them that they are loved and accepted. It reinforces their self-esteem and solidifies their sense of identity. It gives them a sense of commitment and loyalty. They know who they are, who they belong to, where they are from and where they can always be at home.

One father explained this feeling succinctly. He said that for his family, the best time of the day comes just after 6:15 a.m. every morning. This is the time when his three little 'mates' give him a wake-up call. They clamber all over him and his sleeping wife, burrow into the sheets and snuggle close. These parents then tickle them and delight in the squirming little bodies and the screeching little shouts of laughter. After a bit of playing, each child gets a tight little hug from mom and dad. Equipped with two warm kisses and a fiercely loving hug, each child is ready to face the day. So are the parents!

> "It is nice to feel this way early in the morning with their warm little bodies tumbling over us. Such times make me feel that life is good."

This is family feeling – that feeling of warmth and total satisfaction we get when we are with loving, caring family.

So, how can we connect with our children? How do we build this 'family feeling'?

Traditions

Every family has certain traditions and practices that helps it to maintain its identity.

Important rituals and meaningful events act as bonding agents that bring the family together. Some of these rituals are common, others are unique. These traditions, common and unique, instill a sense of belonging in the members. It makes everyone feel like a part of the whole, with a known role to play. Most importantly, it makes each person feel needed, loved and wanted.

> In one family, their best traditions are the weekend picnics at the end of every quarter. Here is Ted and Melissa's story.
>
> Children understand that throughout the year, we are all busy. The two weekends following the close of every quarter, though, are inviolable. We cancel all programs and take off to a vacation spot. These established holidays help us get through the drudgery of the busy months. It is also a time for renewal and growth. We eat our favorite foods, talk late into the night and just do whatever makes everyone happy. We have no agenda except to get connected, share, joke and enjoy.

Vacations and day trips are a great way of bonding, especially with your teens and preteens.

Girls in their preteens are at a particularly touchy stage of their lives. There are all these hormones raging within them. They are unsure of their bodies, and have feelings that need to be worked out. Many of them are ashamed or insecure about the transformation they are undergoing. They do not like to be touched, cuddled or kissed by their parents. They need reassurance, support and understanding more than ever, at this point in time.

One experienced mother of three girls told me that the best way to connect with girls at this stage is a shopping spree, a movie outing or a dinner trip. I agree. Nothing gets a girl more excited than a new tube of lipstick, a bottle of perfume, or a shared pizza!

A family vacation is a bonding experience. The planning, the excitement, the arguments and the packing – they bring the family together. Children who are given the responsibility of taking care of a part of the arrangements become so solemn in their duties that they learn values of responsibility and punctuality, at least temporarily! Some of these trips could be to a zoo, a public garden, a local fair or an exhibition of any kind.

Over the years, some of our trips have been our greatest source of strength and unity. On one such trip with the entire family, we were all stranded near a historical museum, when I suddenly found that I had misplaced my purse. That purse contained car keys, money, credit cards, and who knows what else! We ran in all directions until my son got wise and started organizing us into search parties and deploying us.

The old monument was in ruins and there were so many places we'd visited and roamed through that we did not know where to start searching. Still, we split into groups and went our separate ways. Since I was pretty sure of one spot at the top of a steep hill, I decided to go there. Dru accompanied me.

Halfway up, I stumbled on something and stretched out my hands to break my fall. There, at that moment, my black purse fell on to the ground. Dru and I stood transfixed for a moment, as if we had seen a snake. I had been clutching the purse under my arm on the inside of my coat, and had not realized it. Dru looked at me for a long moment and said, 'Mom, I think you're going to be in BIG trouble." (Sounding uncannily like his grandfather...)

We trudged downhill as fast as we could. I was getting more and more nervous by the minute. Fortunately, when we reached down, everyone else was waiting, with glum faces, as they had found nothing. When I told them what happened, there was a moment of pin drop silence. I could not bring myself to say a thing. Then, somebody laughed – and laughed and laughed. Soon, the others followed and we just couldn't stop laughing.

Even today, when we get together, we talk about how I managed to 'misplace' my purse ... right on my person!

I guess the charm is that despite the fiasco, we had a shared experience that was fun. It was something that we could all look back upon and laugh.

That is what 'family feeling' is all about. That is what some of your best memories will be made of, too.

Sometimes, even something as inconsequential and mundane as eating together can be a powerful renewing experience. You may not know it at that time, but getting together at mealtimes can present you with the ideal opportunity to connect with your growing children.

A friend and colleague shared this story.

> "When I was small, we had a tradition of gathering round the kitchen table for food on weekends. Mom was very particular about that. Nobody was allowed to eat alone. "It's sacrilege", she would say.

So, we all gathered around the table twice a day (breakfast was a hurried affair with the older children eating and running out first and the younger ones getting up late). Lunch and dinner were boisterous affairs, with somebody shouting for the sauce or pepper, mom asking one or the other about their day and the older ones discussing the latest movie in town. That noise and hustle, din and commotion was the heart of our family. We loved it even when we were teasing one another about this or that.

Mom always said that she felt the pulse of our family during those times. We discussed romance, religion, girls, boys, teachers, music and everything under the sun. We cried, laughed and spoke of our heartbreaks at that table. Mom listened and consoled. Dad patted our arm and tried to tame the boys. Everyone had a place and if anyone was absent, he or she was sorely missed.

When I look back at my childhood, those mealtimes stand out.

This tradition continues even today. Mom and dad never eat in their rooms or in front of the TV. When we go over, it is understood that dinner times are family times and that nothing, absolutely nothing, can come in its way. All our kids gather together and it is one big melee of grandparents, parents, uncles, aunts, nephews and nieces. To an outsider, it may look like absolute mayhem but to us, it is nothing short of pure, unadulterated love."

Interestingly, eating together and sharing food is one tradition that seems to have left the average home.

> ➢ A nationwide survey shows that less than 40% of our teenagers have their meals with their family. A whopping 60%

and more eat in their rooms, alone, watching the television or talking or texting on their phone.

In our family, we have this tradition of saying Grace at the dinner table. We hold hands, and there is no particular script. Each person speaks about whatever they feel most grateful about. Some of the words we have spoken in Grace over the years still drift into my mind and bring spontaneous smiles of joy and remembrance.

Celebrations

Celebrations are a great opportunity to get together. To me, birthdays are the most precious opportunities to tell people in the family how special they are. Children love to feel special on their birthdays. It is a time to pamper, nurture, love and indulge. By no means does this have anything to do with spending lots of money on gift. This time together is a gift that money can't buy.

A friend in her forties shared this touching story:

> "When we were young, we didn't have much money. So nobody celebrated much on our birthdays. Heck, what with eight people in the family, there were too many birthdays in a year.
>
> We did not have the money to do anything special or buy anything fancy. But dad loved to celebrate and he disliked the thought of any of us missing out or feeling low on our special day. On our birthdays, our parents would get up quite early and get to work in the kitchen. If you woke up in the morning to the delicious aroma of waffles, cinnamon rolls and cream buns, you knew that we were celebrating a birthday. Those

days, it was a special treat and I now realize that my parents were saving most of the year to make all of us feel special.

Now, with three children of my own, we do things a little differently. We take the birthday boy or girl on a special outing. On that day, she or he gets some spending money and they can ask us to take them anywhere they want, usually there is a special breakfast either at home or at a restaurant. In the evenings, we get together with the grandparents, uncles and aunts to an elaborate dinner followed by games and fun. Since we have three kids in the family, these celebrations come around three times a year. And you know what, my kids really love their special days!"

I think birthdays are the perfect excuse to make your children feel pampered, loved and cherished. It is a great time to reconfirm that you love having them in the family, and for all they bring to your life. Every child is different. Indulge each one and treat each one in the way that makes the child happy. It is not what YOU want or think that matters.

I have a son who loves small intimate celebrations. He gets put out by a large party and lots of people. He likes a mint chocolate ice cream birthday cake and he is in heaven. My daughter, on the other hand, likes to be treated like a princess all day long. She likes a huge party, a spectacular dress and lots of gifts. She wears a "this is my birthday button" and a plastic tiara to school. Each child is different. Tune into your child's desires and wishes and celebrate accordingly.

Capturing Important Memories

This brings me to another important act of renewal. How many times have you witnessed something important in your child's life and left without something tangible to hold onto?

One older father in our parent's club spoke about something that made me realize the importance of taking the time to capture memories:

> "Ours was a late marriage. I met my wife when I was 47. She was 42 at that time. We have three children. My wife's last pregnancy was a complicated one. Somehow, she was very scared when she was carrying our daughter. May be it was what the doctors said about her age – she was 52 at that time or maybe she had a premonition. I don't know what it was.
>
> As the time for the delivery drew nearer, I could feel her getting nervous. Sandra was always big on capturing memories. We already had a dozen albums in the attic showing all of our great moments – our wedding day, the arrival of our children, their Christening, first birthdays, picnics and the like. After the third birthday of our second son, she went and purchased a video cam – the gizmo was quite expensive at that time.
>
> When she went into labor, my wife insisted that I have the cam ready to capture her first moments with our daughter. I did not think much of it at that time. My wife hugged our daughter briefly and called her by the name we had already chosen. It was one of those perfect moments, when everything came together and you feel that life has given you everything you wanted.

> But soon after the delivery, complications set in. Sandra started losing a lot of blood and her condition did not stabilize after that. One complication followed another and she finally succumbed to a massive heart attack five days after the delivery. Today, our 8-year old daughter has only one precious memory of her mother – the video that Sandra insisted we make."

That experience reminds me that tomorrow is not promised to everyone. Today, when we celebrate birthdays, have parties or get together with the extended family, we take our camera along, and thankfully have our cell phones to take pictures as well. We click pictures and we store them away. I store the things that are dear to us and once in a while we bring some of it out and show the children.

I have my children's first teeth, drawing books, lock of hair, baby blanket they wore home from the hospital after their birth, and kiddie shoes. Dru's first drawing of a tree. Matt's and Carly's handprints. The first cards they made. I have all this in my keepsake boxes.

I also periodically write love notes and love letters to my children; in the case something were to happen to me, they would have a precious letter, like the one I cherish from my own mother.

Dru shares this memory:

> "Mom had this habit of keeping everything that she felt was important. She had kept one of the pictures I had drawn and painted of a happy home. I still remember that painting. It was all dark colors; the sky was dark orange and the trees were in the shadows. The house itself was in black – only one window was in bright yellow and I had drawn a squiggly woman and written 'mommy' on it. It was good – as good as a 6-year old's imagination and some extra coaching could make it.

Years later, I was going through some difficult times in my teens. A relationship had failed and I was hurting. I could not bring myself to talk about it. I was harsh with my family, not understanding that their sympathetic looks and whispered talk was just their way of extending support. I used to lock myself up in my room and stay there, just so I could be alone with my pain. Then, one day right after dinner, I saw that picture again.

Mom brought it out along with some other stuff and we somehow got caught in those old memories. It was so funny to see that squiggly woman in the drawing. I also saw my tiny handprints, my lock of hair from my first haircut – and there was much comfort knowing how much I have always been loved.

Later that night – or was it early morning? – when I was in bed, I thought about all the things we had discussed; and I realized how lucky I was to have a supportive family. I saw how absolutely lucky I was to have a mom who wanted to preserve parts of me, just so they could think about those times and be happy. Her love humbled me and it touched me like nothing had ever before. I understood so much about love that night."

Express Your Love

I remember reading this cute little quote somewhere:

> "The love in your heart isn't kept there to stay;
> Love isn't love till you give it away."

As a part of a 'love' strategy, I used to do a lot of little things to help my children feel my warmth in different ways. When my children were young, I used to place little notes in places where they least expected it. Their surprised delight was so beautiful to behold. In fact, the first time I posted a little folded 'love you' note in Carly's lunchbox, she was a bit afraid as she thought I had something to communicate with her teacher. Without opening the note, she took it to her teacher, who opened it, read it and smiled broadly.

With twinkling eyes and a stern expression, the teacher turned to Carly and asked, "Is that so? Did you really do this, Carly?"

My little girl was ready to cry. Seeing her worried expression, the teacher gently pulled her near and showed her what I had written. The note said: "Darling, I am so proud of having you for my daughter. I am missing you and can't wait for you to get back home. I love you, Mom."

We smile over that memory even today. It gave my daughter a warm and fuzzy feeling of being loved and cared for.

Today, my children have grown up. I know they no longer carry lunchboxes or use notebooks. I post little notes in the drawers, on the fridge, on the computer screen and on the floor in the hallway. I text them, message them and email them. Always wanting them to know that I'm thinking of them...

Younger kids love getting mails in the postbox and I have often sent my children little 'love notes' in the mail. I sometimes mail them handmade cards so they receive it on their birthdays. Even a scratched note saying 'I love you' is a magical way of keeping in touch. One day I took the notion to plaster Carly's bedroom door with 'sticky' notes all saying why I loved her and describing the wonderful things about her. She kept the notes on the door for months.

A single parent shared this story:

"My wife passed away when my daughters were 12 and 8 respectively. I knew it hit them hard. My wife loved showing her affection. She always pasted little notes telling the kids something warm, funny or nice. I knew the kids missed that.

My wife's death anniversary falls in February, and because of the sad memories associated with that month, I knew that my girls could never enjoy Valentine's Day. One year, I decided to send them both a card and some flowers for Valentine's Day. They were thrilled. So was I.

It's been six years since we started that practice. I still do it. Only difference: I now add a written note to tell my girls why I love them so much and how lucky I am to have them in my life. This personalizes the gift and I know my girls look forward to reading their notes and getting their flowers. This has helped us to stay in touch, just like my wife would have wanted us to."

Buying your children little surprise gifts makes them feel special. You do not have to buy the costliest items. It is not about the money. What counts is that they realize how you feel.

One important point I would like to make here is that children today are bombarded with a lot of _negative_ messages. Those days when parental love could be taken for granted are gone. Unfortunately, real-life incidents and messages doled out by TV, magazines and ad campaigns can be very effective in molding your child's beliefs. They are in danger of believing that you do not care, understand or sympathize. It is very much a part of your job to convince them of the truth.

HINT: Parenting is all about communicating!

Talking and Conversation

Ever noticed how your child goes from a babbling baby to a highly reticent, secretive even, teenager in the space of 8-15 years? Many parents often tell me that they feel like their teens are speaking a very different language and their children have become the proverbial 'ships passing in the night'.

These changes did not occur overnight. When did the problems start? How did they get that way?

In most cases, parents and children are feeling the same frustrations and dealing with the same anger and pain, without letting the other party in on it. They are both fighting in the darkness, sparring and poking at imaginary hurts. There can be a huge gap in communication. Often what is said is not what is heard; what is meant is not understood … and vice versa. You may be saying the same things that you used to tell your young child, but now whatever you say takes on unintended meanings, have unimagined repercussions, and leave unknown scars on your child's heart.

As children grow, communication patterns need to change and evolve.

Let me cite an example. Suppose you wanted to persuade your reluctant toddler son to take a bath. What would you do? You would think of a strategy that made the child choose what you want. "Would you like a long warm bath in the tub today? Shall we use some of those scented bubbly fizz balls and have some fun?" That's all there is to it, a bath it is!

Now, let us suppose that you wanted your teen-aged son to take a bath. You already know that you cannot use the same strategy there. If you asked him something like "Would you like to try a long bubbly bath in the tub, sweetie?", he would probably give you a stare that spoke volumes and then walk away with a shake of his head!

The strategy you use with your toddler is not going to work with your teen. Teens have an extra pair of antenna with which they can easily detect all your ulterior motives, so forget about hidden agendas. What <u>can</u> you do when the direct approach cannot get you anywhere?

The first thing to do is to remember that your teen has not evolved into "that stranger" all of a sudden. Changes like these do not happen overnight. The breakdown of communication is a slow and gradual process. Never allow this to happen to your family. Here are a number of things you can do, on a regular basis, to keep in touch with your teens:

- ➢ Acknowledge them when they come home. Greet them warmly and make them feel that you are happy to see them. *Stop what you are doing* and give them all your attention – look at them and say 'hello'.

- ➢ Acknowledge your teen when they come into the room or talks to you. Sometimes, our teens do want to talk, but change their minds when they see that we are intent on something else. They know from prior experience that you may only give them half an ear, or worse, brush them off.

- ➢ Whenever your teen goes out, alone or with others, ask where he or she is going. When they come back, ask them how their outing went.

- ➢ Set clear time limits. Ask your teens to get back home before the prescribed hour. If they cannot make it, ask them to call you and check with you. When they are younger teens, wait up for them so they know that you are concerned.

- Ask them how their day went. Encourage them to talk about friends, teachers, class, favorite subjects, feelings and thoughts. A shared evening meal or just a sit-down snack time is a great opportunity for this.

- Keep a close watch on their friends. Most teen problems start with the wrong company; peer pressure can be ferocious. *Know your child's friends.*

- Don't sweat the small stuff. If something is not really important in the long run, let it go. There are phases when your teens feel the urge to act up, and you must decide boundaries and agree upon them.

- Talk to your teens about what they like. If they enjoy reading, talk about some of their favorite books. If they love music, talk to them about their kind of music. Watch their favorite TV shows, go to movies, plays, etc. Facilitate them having good books.

- Allow your teen the thrilling opportunity to teach you something. If they love gaming, try to join them in front of the computer. When you lose, your teen will have some sense of being superior to you. This is also a wonderful opportunity to start a heart-to-heart conversation. Allowing your teen to teach you something is a great heart-warmer.

- Visit them in their bedroom for a short chat just before they turn in. This can become a relaxing and bonding ritual. Remember, your teen is growing; your conversations do not always have to center on your teen. You can discuss issues at your workplace. This will get them interested in talking and finding out more. The objective here is to bond, not to give advice.

With teens, you have to use a mixture of direct conversation and strategizing. Sometimes, clear instructions are the order of the day. "No, you cannot stay out after 11 p.m. Other kids may be doing it, that's between their parents and them. But, you will get home before 11. No exceptions. Got it?"

When dealing with limits, guidelines and expectations must be direct. When you give vague instructions, your child is free to interpret them to suit their purposes. You cannot fault them for it. I post 'rules' on the fridge so that Carly and I both 'remember' what we have agreed on!

So, a wise parent needs to come out with a mixture of both styles – some direct talk interspersed with half-sentences and questions.

The days of long-drawn out philosophical ruminations are over. Your teen is not going to hang on to every word you say and look at you in awe like you are Professor Dumbledore. Those days are well and truly over.

One father I coached describes his experience:

> "There was a time when my boy used to love talking into the wee hours on our camp nights – we used to spend one night every alternate week in a camp in our garden, just him and me. I would finally have to act as if I'd dropped off to sleep to get him to sleep. But things have changed now. Ever since his voice started breaking, he has stopped his chatter. Now he grunts, snorts and hiccups. That's all the answer I can get from him. Sometimes it drives me nuts, but if I address it with him, and ask why he cannot answer in full sentences, he looks at me like I've just walked in from Mars without my clothes on!"

A mother once wrote me this e-mail through www.coachlorna.com:

> "Dear Lorna, my daughter is 17 years old. She has always been a happy child with a lot of talk in her. I used to enjoy listening to her talks while working in the kitchen. Her talk, her expressions, her face and her emotions were a pleasure to watch.
>
> I don't know what got into my daughter recently. Now, she hardly ever talks to me. She is always in her room, listening to music, instant messaging on the computer, and or reading her magazines. When I try to talk to her or ask her about her friends or her life, she talks for about 3-5 minutes and just switches off. It's like she has an internal clock that rings an alarm when she has talked for 5 minutes or so. Then, she just clams up. Can you tell me why this is so? The moment I show interest and ask her questions, she stops talking. It is so frustrating. Sometimes I wonder whether it's something I said!"

No, it is not something you said or did, I explained to the mom. That is just the way teens are. Accept it and be grateful that you had a conversation, even though it was short.

A better part of teenage moodiness is the result of normal developmental processes. They need time to absorb the changes happening around, the new responsibilities that they face, the new information that is trickling down from every direction. In short, your teen's *inner life* is very busy at this time. Thoughts, ideas and opinions are thrashing about in their minds like water in a mighty ocean. So they need more time to sort things out in their minds before they are ready to turn to you.

That also explains why your teenager cannot relate to long conversations anymore. There is too much going on inside their minds. Instead of a long uninterrupted conversation, think in terms of short talks that will set your teen to thinking.

Teens want their parents to listen. What they do not want is a sermon. Young people quite often get unsolicited advice. This is not your fault because you are anxious and you want to help. Your teen is getting to a stage where he or she does not want help. They need a sounding board. It will be a matter of time before this too changes and they will be back seeking your advice.

Talk less and listen more. If you have an opinion to give, just state it and leave it at that. The ideal is to plant the idea casually and leave it, so your child will think that he or she has the power to make a decision. If you push, they will dig deep and refuse to budge. Worse still, they may run the opposite way!

> "So, what do you think you should do for your birthday? Bring the girls here or take them out?"
>
> "Ummm…I don't really know. They would have more fun here because we can talk and chat. But the food would be better over there. I don't know. Let me think about it."
>
> This is your signal to stop. Let it be. But, it might be a good idea to give her a gentle nudge in the direction you want, so she starts an internal dialogue with herself. So you go:
>
> "Sure, you might want to think of a third option too while you're at it."
>
> The next day, while you are watching TV, you may resume, as if there had never been an interruption:

"Did you think about that third option we spoke of?"

"Yeah. Order food. I don't like that idea much. It feels so impersonal. But I want the girls to have fun."

"It's your birthday, you know. What do you think will make YOU happy?"

"You really want to know?"

"Yes."

"I think I'd like some of your chocolate rolls, strawberry tarts and pizza. With lots of pop, of course. But do you think they will like it?"

"I think so. Besides, maybe you can even make it a sleep-over party, if you want to."

"Wow. I hadn't really thought of that. That would be real cool. Thanks mom."

> What makes this approach successful is that while you are influencing her decisions, you do not take away her feeling of responsibility.

This is what most 'almost-there-adults' can't stand, to be taken over, dictated to and reduced to the status of a baby. When your child realizes that you will not be micromanaging his or her life, they may automatically turn to you when they feel the need to. Some of the most helpful responses from a parent to a teen go like this:

- ☆ "You must have thought/felt/ ..."
- ☆ "What did you feel?"

- ☆ "That is really cool/exciting/great news ..."
- ☆ "I am so happy for you ..."
- ☆ "Oh, I know exactly how that feels ..."
- ☆ "And what is your decision? ..."

Your adolescent is not going to grow up in a hurry, you know. So you don't have to get in every concern, every thought and every philosophy in one go. Space it out. Leave some thoughts unspoken. Sometimes, your silence can be your biggest show of support and understanding.

When you move a step back and allow teens the freedom to help set the rhythm of your relationship, you can expect some amazing rewards. There will be unexpected moments of tenderness, open communication and unparalleled vulnerability. There may be moments when your teen suddenly asks you for help, talks to you about something very personal and takes you back to the days before adolescence happened. Treasure these moments because they are few and far in between. Also, do not expect the phase to continue. The next morning may see your teen back on that lonely island, from where she or he made a sudden detour. Be prepared for the distance. Those few moments of tenderness help your child find the strength to face their personal struggles with a straight back and square shoulders.

Doing Things Together

Companionship is a great thing in relationships. Companionship means that you and your child are equal partners. Well, almost... They are free to air their opinions and you are willing to listen to their views and opinions. These are moments of real kinship where there is no power struggle between you and your teen.

Get involved in some favorite activity and ask your teen to join in. Have your teenager join you in making the Sunday brunch or weekend dinner. May be they can decide the menu and go shopping. My daughter loves to do this with me. She makes the menu and we decide what we need. She then takes over the shopping, while I sit back and watch. What always amazes me is that she is very prudent and careful with the money she spends. She also takes special care with what she buys. Since she is making the decisions and the purchase, it goes without saying that she will eat what she buys!

Gardening can also be another great bonding experience. Get together over a pot full of flowers, tomatoes or orchids and start a conversation.

NOTE: Do not try to hog the conversation or impose your thoughts on your teen when you are doing things together or your child will avoid these activities. Instead, use these as opportunities for quiet companionship, fun and laughter. If your teen feels the need to take up something serious, she or he will initiate the conversation.

School projects are another fantastic way to get together and foster the family spirit. Carly once had a school project on Egypt. To us, Egypt meant only one thing at that time – good old Cleopatra! When she started working on the project, we went for a family outing to the local museum. It was a fabulous learning experience for all of us. We went to the library and museum, collected notes, watched TV shows and listened to news clippings. For a month and a half, the entire family had only one mission, to know more about Egypt! In the evenings, we would all get together with printouts and paper clippings and discuss the important features. We would decide what needed to go in and what should be kept out of the project. We helped Carly compile her project. It was a learning experience and a whole lot of fun. We talk about those days even now. "Do you remember that story about the Pharaohs?" or "It's somewhat like that article on the Sphinx, you remember?"

One of my clients once told me this:

> "When my daughter started going to this new school, we thought it would be fun. We knew that they had many art related activities and Emily was really into drawing, painting, decoration and such stuff. But when she started bringing her projects home, we were terrified. I mean, how do you teach a child to paint a picture, and me, with thumbs instead of fingers on both hands!
>
> Finally, after hedging it a little and watching our daughter struggle all by herself, we decided that we had to do something. My wife started scouring the Internet to find easy tips and tricks. We started giving her ideas and listening to her feedback about colors, shading and the like. Many times, we were pleasantly surprised by how much she knew instinctively. This made us realize that Emily was good at this kind of thing, so it was an easy decision to make when she had to choose a career option.
>
> Besides, now we regularly help the children in our neighborhood with their projects. Pot making, weaving, clay modeling, drawing, art, card making, whatever you need, you can count on the Lackner family, that's what our neighbors say!"

The above are a number of things that you can do with the entire family. What if you wanted to spend some extra time with just one person in the family? There must have been times when you felt the need to connect with one particular member of your family. As a young mother with three children, I have often felt the need to go to the top of a mountain and stay there all by myself so I could return rejuvenated in mind and spirit. Research says that this 'alone time' brings in much inner healing. This is true in the case of relationships too.

A wonderful thing happens in a relationship when two human beings spend some time 'absolutely and completely' with one another. You did this when you were newly married. Remember your honeymoon?

After the children come, you get totally embroiled in daily demands. There is always something going on. The result is that you pay attention in half-measures to everyone, but find yourself falling short of your own expectations. You want to do more, but cannot find a way out.

Family one-on-one times are the times when you spend time with any ONE member of your family – your spouse, partner, son or daughter. These offer you exactly the kind of bonding opportunities you are looking for.

> "The best thing about one-on-ones is that you are completely present for the other person. When you are completely present with one person for a limited time, you are willing to suspend your own likes, dislikes, ego and concerns to allow the other person to express his or her own interests and goals. Times like these can play a pivotal role in the shaping of your family life", says Iris, a mother of two children.

Your one-on-one times with your child can include visits to local museums, parks, theatres or an evening at the Opera. It could also be a dinner date or an evening at the ice rink. Nothing can convince your child of your affection and love for them as the time you spend with them – ALONE! Beware, the reverse is equally true.

A mother explains how her one-on-one times with her son helped her make a crucial discovery:

> "I had read somewhere that when children grow up, they feel unsure about a lot of things. Sure enough, when my son started Junior High, I could see that his crystal-clear

perceptions of the world were beginning to cloud. So far, his world was only in black or white. Now the grays had started coming in.

When our son was tense, we would try to make some extra time to be with him. Either my husband would go or I would, and our son knew that the evening was completely his. There were no hidden demands, no reason to talk. He had the freedom to discuss anything he wanted or remain completely silent.

One such evening, my son revealed some disturbing goings-on in his class to my husband. We discovered that one of his closest friends had started teasing him. Our son did not know how to interpret this. He was confused and racked with anger. When he finally blurted out what he felt, there were tears in his eyes.

We resolved that issue within a few days. But what was gratifying, was that our son found it easy to talk to us about it. We realized that he could have hidden the serious issue and gotten himself into deep emotional scarring.

The most important thing we have learnt through the years is that family comes first.

So, when it comes to resolving issues, our motto is this: *Let us create an environment where our son finds it easy to approach us at the very beginning.* That way, we will not have a massive issue that could need months or years of therapy, recuperation and healing. We try and aim to nip distressing events in the bud."

Social service and charity work are leveling experiences that allow your teen to see the world in its true colors. Young children learn more from what they see than from your advice. Take your children to visit a cancer care center or an AIDS care facility. Take them to a drug rehab center. Let them see the patients, hear their stories and understand what they are going through. These kinds of visits are enriching experiences that leave an indelible mark on their young minds. They also allow you to slip your messages into their minds and give you an opportunity to talk about delicate issues.

A friend of mine described how she had been a part of a team that helped female victims of physical abuse. Her children, a son and daughter, regularly helped out with meetings and seminars. Today, her son is a lawyer specializing in criminal law. Even in his mid-thirties, he pitches in to help the victims by offering them free advice and guiding them.

Connecting with your children is important because children thrive in an environment of love. They need constant reassurance because their world is changing incessantly. They come across so many conflicting yet powerful events in life as they grow up. Therefore, it is only natural that they need a firm bedrock of love, affection and unconditional support to get them through these difficult years. At such times, all we can do is be there for our children, give them as much of our time as we can and allow them to *feel* our love. From personal experience, I have found out that this support is difficult to give but it is all that they need to find themselves and emerge as strong individuals.

Exercise:

> ➢ Get your family members to talk about the traditions in your family. Ask them what they like and what they feel needs improvement. (I was pleasantly surprised when my son Matt said that he enjoyed our yearly visit to a particular theme park every summer).

- Discuss activities that bring you together. Plan for regular periodic picnics or events where you can enjoy each other's company.

- Explore opportunities for social service. Talk to your family about the importance of helping people and find out if you can form a team or a group to further some noble cause in the society.

- Crack jokes, play the fool or do whatever it takes to laugh aloud in each other's company.

- Write notes about the positive things you like about each other.

Chapter 5: Self-Esteem, Decoded

"Whatever words we utter should be chosen with care for people will hear them and be influenced by them for good or ill."
- Attributed to the Buddha

"Every word, facial expression, gesture, or action on the part of a parent gives the child some message about self-worth.
It is sad that so many parents don't realize what messages they are sending."
- Virginia Satir

It is so very easy for any human to be negative. To criticize, negatively judge, be cynically snide, to cruelly joke, to sarcastically opine. It is so very uncomfortable for us to realize – through self-observation primarily – that we are not speaking to neutral ears, but destroying a spirit when we are so negative. Especially young children are like sponges to all this negativity. We say we are doing it to "show a kid the error of his ways". Really? There is another way. Use it.

Why? Because there is one asset that young children must absolutely possess if they are to grow into successful individuals. It is a quality that has received a lot of attention in the recent years. Even so, it is a rare quality among children these days.

I am talking about *self-esteem*.

What is self-esteem? A little difficult to define and grasp, self-esteem is *what and how we feel about <u>ourselves</u>*.

It is different from self-confidence and self-image, although these also play an important part in forming your self-esteem. To some, self-esteem is merely a feeling of 'general wellness and happiness'. Others have equated self-esteem with feeling worthy of meeting the challenges of life, of getting on top of any situation and of being absolutely sure of your own limits while accepting them completely.

The truth? Self-esteem is all this and more.

According to the National Association of Self-Esteem, self-esteem is *"the experience of being capable of meeting life's challenges and being worthy of happiness"*. All the emotions you feel when you think of yourself and your abilities are self-esteem.

People with positive self-esteem feel good in their own skin. They are successful in dealing with other people and situations. They go through life in a balanced fashion. They are happy and content. They smile a lot and always carry a feeling of general well-being.

Positive self-esteem is not overconfidence. People with positive self-esteem do not brag; they are not arrogant. They don't need to be. In their own mind, they know how much they are worth. Self-esteem is not about denying flaws and rejecting imperfection. It is knowing that you are worthy of being loved and respected *in spite* of your imperfections.

All of the above is true when it comes to your children, too.

To understand self-esteem a little better, let me tell you a story about a farmer who was famous for growing prize pumpkins. This farmer grew the biggest and the most luscious pumpkins in his country. But one day, the farmer put a growing pumpkin hanging on a vine, into a jar. While the rest of his pumpkins grew bigger and bigger, this pumpkin grew only to the size of the jar.

If you are the pumpkin, that jar is your sense of self-esteem. Can you see how important it is for children to develop the right sense of self-esteem?

Children's perception of themselves plays a major role in everything they do.

It directly affects their performance at school and work, in their relationships and their accomplishments in life. We can go so far as to say that *perceptions shape a child's entire life.*

A friend had this story to share:

> One afternoon as we were picking tomatoes from our garden, I asked my daughter, "Do you know how precious you are to us?"
>
> "Yes mom. I know you love me more than your diamond ring." The quick reply caught me off guard.
>
> "Honey, what does what I feel for you have to do with my diamond ring?"
>
> "When you misplace your ring, you become upset. You worry and fret until you find it. And when you find it, you give the ring a big kiss."
>
> "Yes, and so?" I asked struggling to see the connection here.
>
> "That's exactly what happens when I'm late in getting home. You even say the same words." Ooops ... This was getting interesting.
>
> "Like what?" I asked.

> "Don't ever do that to me again", came the pat reply, dramatics and all.
>
> "I really say that?"
>
> "Yes", my daughter affirmed solemnly, "and then you give me a big kiss!!"

Notice how this child had picked up on associations that adults totally miss? That's children for you!

Before we can understand how we can help our child develop positive self-esteem, it is important to make a vital distinction between *fact* and *perception* or *information* and *evaluation*.

> A *fact* is a piece of data that is backed by objective evidence. It is universal and cannot be readily challenged.
>
> An opinion, on the other hand, is a conscious or unconscious *perception* formed by a person. It is highly subjective and is therefore inclined to be wrong, mistaken, inaccurate and biased.
>
> *Information* is a neutral piece of data, and may or may not be a *fact*. *Evaluation* is never neutral, but positive or negative based on the evaluator's *perceptions*.

So, you see, the ideas children form about themselves are NOT facts even though they may seem like it. They are not rooted in reality but they <u>appear very real</u> to young minds.

Low self-esteem starts developing very, very early in childhood, when a young and vulnerable child first forms an initial view of the world and 'fixes' their place in it. Children start to form their self-esteem – positive or negative – very young. They test their environment and form *feelings and opinions* about themselves that are reinforced in later life.

Newborn children develop their sense of self as early as 3-6 months in life. For example, when the child cries and a parent rushes to pick it up, the child understands that it is worthy of love. The next time a similar sequence of events takes place, the child's sense of trust, security and self-importance gets a positive boost. When more such events take place to boost the naturally buoyant feelings of self-worth, the child develops positive self-esteem.

Please note that what the child *perceives* may be different from absolute reality. A parent may be unavailable to attend to the child's call or may be unwilling to spoil the child. This topic fills many books with advice to parents – and it is up to each parent to decide what their 'truth' is as far as responding to the cry of a baby.

Self-esteem grows and changes every day in young children. Their sense of 'self' evolves from the various experiences they have in life. They are continuously making adjustments to their quota of self-esteem through the feedback they receive from people around them – and through their personal evaluation/interpretation of that feedback.

As children learn and master new skills, their self-esteem develops. As they try, fail, try again and accomplish what they set out to do, they are constantly checking out their limits. Interactions with people help the child form their self-concept. A positive self-esteem is an armor that enables the child to face the trials of life. It is a measure of the child's maturity and character. It develops mostly in childhood.

When desirable reactions do not follow instantaneously, children start suspecting that they have done something to deserve rejection. They feel responsible. Thus begins the long and complicated story of negative self-esteem.

Imagine for a moment that a child's self-esteem is a savings bank account. Every incident that strengthens their self-esteem is an investment. Any incident that shatters their happy notions of themselves is a withdrawal from the bank account.

Here's the catch: Every deposit is <u>small</u>; every withdrawal is <u>heavy</u>. Therefore, self-esteem grows slowly, but it can be shattered in one cruel blow.

When children feel happy, capable and worthy, they become confident. Children with positive self-esteem:

- Assume responsibility
- Feel proud of themselves and their achievements
- Are independent
- Are self-reliant
- Are comfortable in interactions with others
- Tolerate frustration in a positive manner
- Are not devastated by failure
- Take on new challenges enthusiastically
- Assist others
- Resist bullying or are individuals that never attract it
- Resist becoming a victim
- Handle positive and negative feedback with equanimity – bounce back quickly from a setback
- Are generally cheerful

Parental influence accounts for a great amount of a child's evaluation of self. Naturally, parents are the first influences that act upon a growing child. They are also the most powerful, both emotionally and psychologically.

Research shows that four important areas of parental behavior influence a child's self-esteem:

1. The degree of approval, acceptance and affection parents and caretakers show towards their children.

2. The extent to which clear standards of behavior have been set by parents and caretakers, and met by children.

3. The extent to which discipline was based on logical explanation of limits rather than coercion or force.

4. The extent to which children were encouraged to contribute to solving family problems.

The interesting relationship between low self-esteem and the lack of clear-cut standards of discipline is worth mentioning.

Often, teens who are allowed to 'go completely wild' as they go through their teen years, become individuals with 'bloated' self-esteem. And bloated self-esteem is not healthy, as it is really more of an arrogance. They come to arrogantly over-estimate their abilities and worth to the possible extent of putting others down.

To understand the role of discipline in success and life, let me relate a short story.

> A young boy was flying a kite with his father. On that windy afternoon, the boy's kite was flying high up in the sky, tugging at the string with all its might. The boy was barely able to hold the kite in check with the string. So he asked his father, "Dad, why don't we cut off the string? Won't the kite fly higher then?"

The wise father smiled and cut off the string. Just as the boy had predicted, the kite soared higher. After some time, it got entangled in a tree and fell to the ground.

That string is *discipline*. Discipline is the string that ties us to reality and gives us our sense of orientation. Without it, we may soar for a time, but we ultimately crash against obstacles and fall.

Discipline is loving firmness. Children need discipline and accountability even if they appear to not like it. It is important to give choices to your children, but choices without limits and freedom without direction and consequences can be dangerous.

Children with a bloated sense of self feel that the world owes them everything. Such children put on a false sense of bravado even if they are crumbling inside. In the end, they lead a life of unmitigated loneliness and sorrow. The negative feedback they receive bogs them down. They feel misunderstood, dissatisfied and disappointed. In short, they become square pegs that will never fit into round holes.

Another interesting factor seems to be that a small but significant part of self-esteem is inherited, which means that if parents suffer from symptoms of low self-esteem, it seems their children have a higher chance of developing negative self-esteem.

Some of the most common reasons for frail self-esteem in children are:

> ➤ Parents who have unrealistic expectations naturally criticize the child too much. Words mold a child's world. They create the child's sense of reality. When they begin to feel that they can never measure up, they feel worthless and insecure.

- Parental abuse (constant scolding, yelling, hitting and harsh punishments) hurts the children in more ways than one. These children become adults who have been 'brainwashed' with negative and self-defeating messages, like 'Lazy Lucy', 'Your middle name is Irresponsible', 'What are you good for, anyway?', 'How foolish can you get?', 'Where's your brain? Did it fall out?', 'Listen up, airhead', 'How many times do I have to tell your pea-brain?', or 'You're so stupid!'

- Lack of adequate verbal and behavioral affection can belittle the child and make him feel insecure and unimportant.

- Sometimes parents poke fun at their children, not with an intention to hurt, but to amuse themselves. Nobody likes to be the butt of family jokes. Some of the barbs inevitably hit home, fester and lead to poor sense of self-worth.

- Children need affirmation of their opinions, ideas and thoughts. How other people react to us, whether they reject, condemn, criticize, deride or ignore our ideas, forms the basis of how we feel about ourselves.

- Emotional unavailability of parents makes children insecure. Parents may be too busy or uninterested to care; or they may shy away from physical demonstration of love. The absence of adequate reassurance, love, warmth and security can lead to a distorted sense of self.

- Unfair comparisons can also question a child's sense of self. Comparisons with better achievers – be it a sibling, friend, classmate or neighbor – chips away at the child's positive sense of self.

- Related to the above, how many kids get a 'family label?' One child is 'our artistic son', another is 'our math whizz-kid', while another is 'our dreamer' and so on. Why limit your kids, however loving and well-intended, with any label?

- When children are left alone to deal with difficult situations like a divorce, an accident or a mishap, they feel afraid and let down. They also feel responsible, unsure and afraid. Unavailability of a gentle guiding force leads to a heavy withdrawal from the child's self-esteem account.

- Threatening to punish the child with punishments they cannot fathom can make the child withdraw. Threatening to abandon the child, disown them, give them up for adoption, send them off to boarding school, or lock them up without dinner, chips away at their self-esteem.

- Sometimes, parents hold their children back from normal activities. They may have their reasons for it. However, not being allowed to participate in normal fun activities can be a blow to a child's fledgling sense of self.

- Parenting styles influence a child's sense of self-esteem. If you are uninvolved, authoritarian or permissive, your children can develop symptoms of negative self-worth.

- Family conflicts, unresolved problems and family breakdown also damage a child's sense of self and his sense of belonging. This does not mean that parents should hide all signs of conflict from their children. Children need to see healthy arguments. They also need to witness healthy resolution of problems. This makes them learn important life skills. Such children are better able to cope with disagreements later on in life.

➢ Some children feel inferior because they lack appropriate social skills. When such children attract the wrong kind of attention, it forces them into a tight cocoon of pain, withdrawal and hurt. To avoid this pain, they try to erase themselves and merge into the background. This is an important symptom of low self-esteem.

➢ Serious diseases or medical conditions can lead to low self-esteem. Learning disorders, child diabetes and other such conditions make the child feel that he is 'not normal'.

➢ Sometimes, social pressure can make the child feel inadequate. Belonging to a poor, drunken or destitute family will have a major impact on a child's sense of self. Children who are born to such parents often struggle with their self-image for a long time.

How does low self-esteem affect children and young adults?

Low or negative self-esteem is not much of a problem in early infancy. It becomes a matter of great concern as a child begins school and enters the world of social interactions. Once low self-esteem establishes itself in the mind, it becomes the child's reality.

One worried mother wrote me this letter:

> "My daughter Tanya is a shy, quiet child of 12 who loves to read. In the evenings when most of her friends are busy with their games, she sits at home with a book. I often sweet-talk her into going out and playing with her friends. Occasionally, she agrees and goes out to please me.
>
> But once outside, Tanya finds it difficult to join the group. She waits to be invited. Obviously, that is going to be difficult. Sometimes, when she is invited to join, her contribution to the

game is minimal. She keeps herself as far away from the action as possible. After some time, she gets bored and walks away from the game without even saying goodbye to her friends. Her friends also do not miss her when she quietly walks away from the game.

Tanya comes home in tears. She blames me because she now feels worse than before. Why is this happening? She is a bright and pretty young girl. Why is she finding it so difficult to belong?"

Children learn to value themselves only as much as they are valued. Tanya's mom might not realize it, but the child's negative self-esteem has taken control of her. Every time she feels rejected and hurt, her low sense of self-worth is reinforced.

Children who have low or negative self-esteem may show:

- Fear or disinterest when it comes to learning new things
- Symptoms of inadequacy when compared to friends or siblings
- Emotional and physical withdrawal
- Aggression, anger or frustration
- Fear of expressing their opinions
- Guarded behavior, limited interactions
- Pandering to the wishes of others
- Tendency to develop dangerous behavioral patterns like self-harm, sexual aberrations, drug addiction, cutting, violent tendencies and a total disregard for rules.

What is so painful is that many of these characteristics are self-actualizing.

How Can Parents Help Repair the Damage?

Young children need to grow in an atmosphere of approval, love and encouragement. They thrive when they meet with *deserving* approval. The ties children form during infancy develop and strengthen over time.

As a rule, small children are always eager to please. Getting a new task done gives them immense satisfaction. Feeling capable of accomplishing something is very important for the development of positive self-esteem. Through this, children experience self-satisfaction and develop a positive view of the self. This is how their self-esteem grows.

When children reach their preteens, they become more curious. By then, they would already have formed a good worldview. During these years, children want to feel loved and accepted. At this crucial time, you are preparing your children to face their turbulent adolescence, which is just around the corner.

During this period, brace yourself! Your children will ask many uncomfortable questions! Parents need to enlighten children on matters of morality, alcohol, drug abuse and consensual, safe sex, as well as how to act in certain new relationships. It's time for 'the bees and the birds' story to disappear. It is better to discuss uncomfortable topics before they become too difficult to handle. Gaining knowledge and sharing perturbing questions with a parent reassures your child. It also helps dispel a number of myths they may have accidentally picked up.

As children develop, you have to encourage their decision-making skills. In order to train them to do this, allow them to make small decisions, like choosing one game out of two or three, or choosing one item for dinner from a list of two or three. Older children can get involved in more serious decision-making processes, like where to go for a vacation, how to use money wisely, what cereal to buy at the grocery store, etc.

When my middle son Matt was 7 years old, he started to receive his weekly allowance. On the first day of this new and exciting phase, I took him to a flea market. Matt was the excitable one of my brood. He always wanted to spend his money as soon as he got it, while the others liked to save. Of course, Matt was also generous to a fault and he had no qualms in sharing whatever he bought.

On his first visit to the market, Matt saw a bright yellow truck and immediately wanted to have it. The truck was not well-made and I knew that it would not last too long. So I asked Matt to look at how the truck was made and compare it with the trucks he had at home. I did not want to reject his choice explicitly because I wanted him to understand that it was his money and I wanted him to take control of his spending decisions.

After listening to my comments, Matt still wanted the truck. I guess it was a case of falling in love at first sight. So he bought it with his money. Needless to say, the truck did not live long enough to make its way to our home. Matt was heartbroken and sad, as I knew he would be.

This gave me a chance to explain to my 7-year old about certain choices. I talked about *value versus cost* and made him see how his own choices had brought him sadness.

Since I wanted Matt to take control of the situation, I suggested that he could go back to the flea market and talk to the man who sold him the truck. He could plead his case and get a new truck or try ask for a credit to buy something new.

So, off we went to the flea market the next week with the broken truck and an excited and determined Matt in tow. We searched the entire place, but the vendor seemed to have vanished. Matt learned another valuable lesson about second chances.

Today, Matt is 34 and he still remembers the lesson he learned. Of course, today when we talk about it we laugh and shake our heads! At that time, I knew Matt would have changed his decision if I had put my foot down.

> *Children need to exercise their 'choice muscles'*
> *on their own if they are to make*
> *sound decisions when they grow up.*

I believe that, as parents, the first thing we have to teach our children is to take control of their lives, in small steps. We all make mistakes, so be prepared for your child to falter. When they do, we have to be there to support them and guide them towards what they could have done to avoid their mistakes. We need to move them away from their anguish of doing wrong and towards proactive thinking. As a parent, my toughest lesson was to learn to bite my tongue and keep myself from saying 'I told you so'. Being smug at being right is a door closer!

Self-esteem plays a major role in the decisions teenagers make, in the way they act, and the way they develop. Teenage is a period of great turbulence. Excruciating concern over physical appearances is a part of puberty. Changing body shapes, pimples, acne, hair springing up in unexpected places, cracking voice, awkward body movements, it's a whole new world for them. They spend hours in front of the mirror, pirouetting this way and that, trying out make-up and hair gel. All this effort to look good! It might seem strange to you, but appearance is a real concern for your teen.

When teenagers are unhappy with the way they look, self-esteem can take quite a beating. As a general rule, few teenagers are happy with their looks. It takes them a good while to learn that good looks come from *self*-acceptance and *self*-approval, not from commentary of other people. So young teens will have some self-esteem deficit in their account.

When your children are young, it is comparatively easier to find out what is happening. Out of their natural curiosity, they are likely to confide in you. You get an opportunity to talk to them and explain what is happening. You are able to stop more damage. When teenagers have already developed a measure of low self-esteem, the negative cycle can continue for many years without your being able to do something constructive about it.

Teenagers struggle to arrive at their own identities and answers. In their quest for individuality, they distance themselves from people who fret over them the most. This is their way of separating the "I" from the "We". This is what makes most teenagers inaccessible and rebellious.

One father spoke about his own teenage turbulence:

> "I loved music when I was young. It was my identity. One night, when I was practicing for the night's show, one of my friends came running into the hall and showed me a picture of myself playing the guitar. I grabbed the picture, took one look at it and shoved it into my pocket.
>
> For the rest of the day, I was grumpy and depressed. I hated that picture. The chunky roly-poly guy smiling back at me with his pink cheeks and fat arms made me feel like a failure. I wanted to be a rock star. Whoever heard of a fat rock star?
>
> At 200 pounds, I was obese. I hated being the funny guy. I wanted to be the cool dude. I was tired of being overweight.

Finally, I decided to do something about my weight problem. I knew that if I could eat less, I would weigh less. It was difficult, but I started cutting back. I rejected all the fatty stuff, accepted fruits, vegetables and protein. On the weight front, things were looking up or rather going down. I had shed several pounds, and I was delighted.

When I walked into class the next year, I was a new person. Nobody could quite believe that I was the same chubby chap. I finally had chest instead of man boobs, and I could tell where my Adam's apple was. The girls were impressed. I was getting many compliments

My success went straight to my head. Now I was on a roll and I decided to eat just a little less so that I could knock off the last few pounds.

My parents and some of my friends were getting a little worried. My mother often offered me heaped platefuls of chicken and salad. She would sit with me, pretending to chat, while I ate the whole thing. When I had finished, she would happily clear my plate and leave me alone.

I knew her ploy and I wanted to please her. But one day, after eating a plateful of lasagna, I started feeling terrible. Thinking about all the calories I had just put inside made me break out in sweat. I felt as if the food was pushing itself against my throat. Then I felt angry that my mother had tried to force me to eat.

In anger and frustration, I went up to my room to get some rest. The fear, anger and the food inside worked together. In less than five minutes, I was sick. I threw up everything I had eaten. Instantly, I felt weak ... but better. All the calories had come out. That was a neat trick!

From then on, secret activities in the bathroom became a regular feature of my life. I felt as if I were in total control.

Early that spring, I was practicing for a competition. A music company wanted to select some talented players for their amateur music group. I was a good player and I knew I stood a fairly good chance.

I cleared the first two rounds. In the last and final round, there was a panel of five to six people. They did not ask me to play that day. Instead, they asked me a lot of questions about my life. I felt, at the end of the interview, that I have done quite well for myself. Just as I got up to leave, one of the ladies asked me, *"Are you anorexic? Do you have an eating problem?"*

I was caught on the wrong foot and mumbled some trash about healthy eating. I guess they sensed the truth. I could feel the sudden change in the atmosphere. Some looked at me with sympathy while others seemed angry. I remember thinking,' *Hey, what did I do? It's my* body*!'* I knew then that I had lost it. That was the end of my dream.

However, it took me many more years to realize that I had a problem. It took me even longer to understand the root cause of my problem. Unlike what I had believed, I did not have a weight problem; I had a self-esteem problem".

Teens and Self-Esteem Problems

Teenagers often worry about how they look. The better they feel about themselves the higher will their self-esteem be. The higher their self-esteem the better they cope. It is natural for a teen to want to change something in themselves. If that is what your child wants, help them go about it in a positive and healthy manner. Help them set realistic goals. Talk about the importance of health.

Never, ever, make fun of the physical appearance of your child/teenager. Even if it is said as a joke and is meant in a light-hearted way, it likely will hit home. When your child seems particularly troubled about something, it doesn't help to make fun or to take it lightly. They may have very real fears regarding their 'attraction quotient'. Allow your children to express their fears. Listen to them, try to understand how they feel and tell them gently what you think.

If your child colors their hair or gets a wild haircut, gets a weird tattoo or a nose piercing – don't fly off the handle! That will do more harm than good, take it from me. Your children need to experiment with their bodies. Try to accept this and convey your disapproval in a gentle and friendly manner. Something like this:

> "Oh, that looks interesting. I didn't know they made that shade these days! It's nice, but I hope you won't lose the rich texture of your natural hair with too much coloring."

If your child agonizes over pimples, acne, or unwanted facial hair, take them to your doctor to see if they can be helped.

As much as you can, help your teenagers understand that many things about their physical appearance make them unique. The color of their eyes, height, body shape and face are all unique to one special person: your child. Tell them that people rarely notice the minute details that we notice in ourselves. Assure your children that they are worthy and attractive human beings.

Cleanliness and hygiene issues can be another big problem when it comes to teenagers. Hormones change; body odor becomes a bigger deal than when your reluctant bather was 8 years old.

Tidiness of one's person but also with one's possessions might also become an issue. Your teen will own more stuff; make him or her accountable for not only taking care of it, but keeping their space in the home organized as well.

Parents often have to fight with their teenager to ensure tidiness at home. You might not like the idea of picking up after them – so don't! Teach them care of their possessions and respect for the spaces of the home. Kids are never too young to learn these things.

Having said so much already, there may be times when the path of least resistance is the best path. Sometimes, children are not doing these types of irritating things purposely. Their mind may be preoccupied with too many other thoughts. Tidiness is the last thing on their agenda. Try to guide them gently back. At times, learn to turn a blind eye. Do not harp, nag and criticize. This only alienates them. Sometimes with Carly, I will take a cup of tea to her room and sit with her as she 'cleans' her room. It is always a good sharing time, and I always see results by the time my tea is finished.

Teens need lots of personal space. Respect that. Things are bound to be much smoother if you accept the fact that their rooms, books and personal diaries or letters are out of bounds to you. So long as their posters, books, magazines, playing gear and other clutter – whatever it is that makes them feel complete – are within a closed room, shut the door and forget about it. It doesn't help to fret. Your teenager needs some space of their own and they will resist if you try to make 'his' or 'her' space an extension of your own. Young adults need their privacy to enjoy the exquisite agony of a broken heart or a new love, to explore new ideas and act like the crazy kids they sometimes want to be.

Ideally, your teenager should be used to helping with chores around the house. That's what I call 'house training' your kids. To be successful, start early, as has been noted in earlier chapters of this book. If you have not done that, don't expect your children to suddenly become aware of their responsibilities.

Teenage is a time for rebellion when they do NOT like being ordered around. They still need to contribute to household chores. Find out what they like to do through a discussion and get them to perform the kind of chores they like. Once they chose a job, make your expectations clear. If needed, explain what has to be done. Then, leave them to carry out their work. If they come to you for help, assist them. But, do NOT cluck around them like an excited mother hen. Unwarranted interference only makes them feel unsure.

Say 'Thank you' and 'Hey, well done!' Always make it a point to thank your child sincerely for their efforts. In this way, you acknowledge not only their work, but also that they are crossing over from childhood to adulthood.

> **NOTE:** Do not go overboard with praise; be sure to give it when it is deserved; be sure to be specific about what it is that has made you proud, happy or worth mentioning. Be sincere, not grudging or fudging the reality. Kids have a fine-tuned 'BS meter', as they'd call it, and will know when you are trying for 'Political Correctness' rather than real appreciation.

In spite of all your patience, tolerance and understanding, there will be times when things go wrong and everybody feels upset. Confrontations cannot be avoided altogether. Establish rules for the way you expect your teen to speak and behave when there is a disagreement. Make realistic demands and do not give in to teenage tantrums. Here are some helpful to do's:

- Keep communication lines and doors open with them.
- Be calm.

- Don't sweat the small stuff. Sometimes you're the one feeling grumpy ('I want what I want when I want it – because I'M the PARENT!'), so just back off.
- Remember: sometimes, it is just bad luck, not their fault.
- Your teenager needs to be trusted and respected. They like that you tell them the task or goal; they don't like when you give them a blow-by-blow process on how to do it! Understand that they can figure it out!
- Do not label your teenager ('the grumpy one', 'the shouter', etc.)
- If you can't say something nice, it's probably better to keep quiet. Even with plenty of reasons to find fault with your teenager, it is wise to abstain from disparaging remarks when your teen is bristling with an extra helping of ego.
- Introduce your teen to various activities. Remember the old adage – 'an idle mind is a devil's workshop'. A teenager with too much free time will get bored and may look for unhealthy means to relieve their monotony. Pursuits such as camping, trips to the theatre, galleries, museum, watching a good movie together, dance lessons and tennis classes will give them a wide variety of choices. It will keep them busy, but – even more – it will help them discover new talents and skills, while their self-esteem gets a healthy boost.

Self-esteem is a quality that dips and peaks throughout the teenage years. Sometimes, teens are very happy and excited, and sometimes for no apparent reason, they are in the doldrums. Our first duty as parents is to support them in whatever decisions they make, and allow them the room to feel their emotions if things go right or wrong. Some of these decisions may be downright wrong, but if they persist in following through, there is nothing you can do about it, except be there for them when they get hurt.

Chapter 6: Building Rapport or Keeping the Lines of Communication Wide Open

"The single biggest problem in communication is the illusion that it has taken place."
- George Bernard Shaw

"The most important thing in communication is hearing what isn't said."
- Peter Drucker

Two of the things we rarely learn about in school (besides parenting, of course) are how to manage money and how to understand people well enough that we can actually have a meaningful conversation with just about anybody, anywhere, of any age. Public speaking is not the only area where people are uncomfortable talking to someone else. Just look in any family! Let's look at two types of relationship to illustrate.

1st Relationship:

Have you ever been so in sync with a person that you felt like you are an extension of the other person? Think about such a relationship in your life. It could be with your spouse, parent, sibling, friend or business associate. It could be with someone you've known for a long time or it could even be with a stranger you met on a train. Whoever it is, it has to be a relationship in which you never felt the need to be something other than yourself; where there was no need for pretense or explanations; where there was no room for misunderstandings or excuses; where silences filled your heart with pleasure and words that you spoke came from somewhere deep within your spirit.

That feels good, right?

2nd Relationship:

Now think about another relationship – a difficult one which really takes the energy from you; where you to walk on eggshells practically all the time; where every word has to be weighed, calculated and mulled over before it leaves your mouth; where you'd rather take a shuttle to the moon than be in the same room with all that drama and tension ... and that person.

These are two extremes and each one of us experiences them at some point or another. And whether you believe it or not, a large percentage of parent-teen relationship falls in the second category!

I remember reading somewhere that love is a *verb*.

How true this is but how many of us look at it that way? Most of us are brainwashed by popular media into believing that love is an instant spark that lights our hearts. Hollywood has successfully made us believe that love is a magical emotion that suddenly lights your heart and that it is here to stay. But this is not true. In real life, 'happily ever afters are difficult to come by, and take lots of work to accomplish.

Most relationship begins with a firework of some type of explosive passion or the certainty of some real connection. Then, after some time, the passion inevitably subsides; the connection seems to have evaporated. From then on, keeping the relationship alive requires hard work.

This can be true of any lasting partnership with another human being, be it your child, spouse, business associates or friend. Understanding, cooperation and acceptance are the building blocks of a successful relationship and it comes only when BOTH parties are willing enough to WORK for it.

As children move towards their teenage years, parents and teens often gravitate towards the opposite ends of the boxing ring. To an extent, I think this is natural. Up until now, your child has been in your shadow, listening to most of what you say. Then all of a sudden, new dynamics enter into the equation. Your child becomes a new person, his own person. First, there is a burgeoning ego to handle. Then there is that most irritating 'I know it all' attitude and an unwillingness to talk or listen. For a parent, this cauldron of challenging opposites is mystifying and painful. At times, it is difficult to reconcile the prickly, passionate, moody human being in front of you with the lovable and pliable child of yesteryears. Whatever happened to the little champ who used to shed copious tears when you frowned, you wonder! It is especially difficult if you have other children that you are raising at the same time.

The magic of love comes alive when there is cooperation, love and togetherness even in the face of stiff opposition; when the entire family moves forward as a group in spite of differences.

This is where a Family Mission Statement can be an enormous help. On those days when teens decide to be particularly difficult, and when emotions are rubbing you raw, your family mission statement could perhaps be the only resource that sustains you and urges you to keep going. That, and a little faith in the larger picture is what a parent needs during times of crises.

I once heard a story from Carly's school principal that has stayed with me over the years and given me immeasurable amounts of inspiration. I think every parent will benefit from the simple moral in it.

Once upon a time, a man was so frustrated with his life that he decided to give it up. The man trudged to the top of a lonely mountain, where he called God and announced his intention to jump.

Miraculously, just as the man was about to take the leap, a soothing voice came from above. "Son, why do you wish to give up on life?" the voice asked.

"Why should I not? I have been trying all my life to become a successful and happy man. Now I understand that this will never be. Can you give me one reason why I should not give up on my life?" the man asked dejectedly and angrily.

"Son, let me tell you about the first time I planted some plants in my garden. On one side of my garden, I planted a fern plant. On the other side, I planted a bamboo plant. Every day, I would water both the plants; I'd give them adequate nutrients and protection so they could grow and flourish. Every morning, I would go and look at both sides with immense curiosity.

The ferns were the first to show signs of life. A new leaf appeared in a week, followed by another and then another. After a month, the ferns were thriving with new tendrils of lush growth appearing everywhere.

On the other side of the garden, my bamboo plant did not show any sign of life. Not a leaf or shoot made an appearance. That did not deter me, though. I continued to water both my plants just as before.

At the end of the first year, the ferns had spread all over their side of the garden. The fresh green leaves now started making ambitious moves towards the garden walls. I loved their green freshness and their verdant growth. I felt rewarded and happy.

The other side of my garden remained mysteriously quite. My bamboo plant had not grown an inch. There were no new leaves or any sign of life on that side. Nevertheless, I refused to give up on my little sapling. I watered it and nurtured it just the same as before. I spoke to it and looked upon that tiny sapling with all the love in my heart.

A year rolled by and the ferns were growing lusciously. They now formed a green, velvety carpet on their side of the garden. But the bamboo plant was quieter than ever before.

Still I continued to take care of both sides of the garden. I loved my bamboo sapling just as I loved the gorgeous ferns. I watered the bamboo plant, gave it food and cared for it just as before. I did not give up on my plant just because it was not developing the way I wanted it to.

In the third year, the bamboo suddenly showed signs of life. Numerous leaves appeared all of a sudden. The tiny shoot started shooting skywards. In a short span of time, my bamboo plant had grown taller and stronger than the delicate vines of fern. The canopy it formed became the most attractive thing in my garden. Birds came and built their nests on the bamboo tree. There was sweet melody all around because I refused to give up on my bamboo plant", the voice ended.

The man was puzzled and he asked, "Why did you not cut the sapling at first? Why did you let it live?"

The voice replied gently, "My son, in the three years that the plant showed no outward signs of life, my little sapling was growing *underneath* the ground. Deep inside the earth, the plant was busy developing massive root structures that penetrated deep and wide. In all these years, it was preparing itself for the massive growth above the ground. My son, if I had cut the sapling when it refused to grow as I wanted it to, I would have actually killed the plant, which was quietly doing its work.

Is this not reason enough for you not to give up on your life? Is this not reason enough for you to go back and continue with your struggles? In all the years that the fruits are not forthcoming, remember, your plant is growing roots."

As a parent, whenever I have had to face complex problems and emotional roadblocks, I keep going back to that story. I try to believe that my children are still growing their roots. That belief is enough to bring me back to the path of a proactive parent.

Every parent knows how difficult it is to be patient when children are trying their best to thwart you. You need a lot of patience and understanding to carry on in such situations.

Have you noticed that there are some parents who seem to ease into their children's teens? These parents are their children's best buddies, whatever their age. The familiarity and warmth between these parents and their children is amazing: the good news is that you can develop it, too. Yes, you read that right: you CAN develop rapport with your difficult teen.

Without rapport, your chances of effective communication with your children go down by 95%. Rapport is what cements relationships. It is what keeps the engine of interpersonal relationships running smoothly. Without rapport your personal life will be in shambles, relationship with your partner will be dissatisfying and your 'connection' with your children will be nil.

So, what is rapport?

When you have good rapport, you are finding similarities with the person you are communicating with, speaking the same language, looking at things in a similar way. When you have this link, you know where the other person is coming from and you both know what you want.

The key to establishing positive relationships is to understand what the other person is all about, in this case your children.

Before you communicate, ask yourself these questions:

- What are their needs and desires?
- What drives their action?
- What do they want from you?
- What are their expectations?
- What outcome do you want from your conversation?

Once you pause to consider these questions, you're well on your way to understanding your children. Understanding the other person is what rapport is all about!

So, how does rapport feel? Actually, it feels divinely *comfortable*. Rapport is that deeply satisfying feeling of oneness with your child. It is that instinctive spark of connection that sometimes links two people. It is the feeling of 'we', not 'they'. It is that feeling when you chime in, "I know exactly what you mean!" or "I feel the same!"

To achieve rapport, however, it is important to understand one fundamental factor.

*Everybody has a particular map of the world.
This map is their interpretation of
the world outside.*

*You have rapport when you understand
another person's map of the world around them.*

Your map is unique to you and your children's maps are unique to them. No one else can quite catch the subtleties of one person's perception of reality.

Understanding this vital concept is the key to accepting your child wholeheartedly and unconditionally. Remember, you can NEVER see the world as they see it and vice versa.

It is a shared perception of the world outside, where you have a mutual understanding of each other's territory. You understand, so you do not judge.

Mutual understanding is the basis of all relationships. To quite a large extent, we like people who are like us. By the same yardstick, we are inherently suspicious of those who are different from us. This is a universal truth and this applies to your equation with your children too. If you keep pulling them up and demanding that they conform to your view of the world, things are bound to head for a crash.

Establishing rapport with your children is important because it means that things will most likely be easier and smoother in the family. When people have rapport, they respond easily to each other in a friendly and loving manner. They work together, even when they understand the differences between them.
One father shared this story:

"I used to be quite abrupt, gruff and loud with my kids. One day, when my little daughter Kylie was pestering me, I snapped at her. As I turned away, I did not notice the tears in my daughter's eyes. That night, Kylie had a nightmare and she awoke from her sleep screaming.

Later, she told us that in her dream, she saw a bear running towards her ready to eat her. And she said that the bear looked like Daddy, when he was angry.

That comparison shook me. I knew that I was harsh and gruff. I did not know that it effected my daughter so deeply. From that day on, I set out to understand my daughter and to appreciate her point of view before I reacted.

This has made such a difference in my family!

I now use a softer tone of voice and try not to dominate the charming women in my household. But you know what the best thing is? I finally realize that when I have stopped shouting and yelling, I am hearing more. Now, I can hear the nuances in my wife's speech and I know when she is smiling even without looking at her. I know from the way my daughter talks if she's had a bad or good day. And that's just fantastic!"

THAT'S exactly what rapport is. This said, how can you create rapport in your family?

Listen and listen hard. Sometimes when teens are 'bouncing off the walls' and jumping straight at your head, listening might be the last thing you want to do. When words are exchanged in anger and people are hurt, a lot of negative talk is natural. And this happens both ways, from parent to teen and vice versa. Curiously, these are the words we often remember the most.

However, to develop rapport, a parent must learn to listen to the right message. Allow your teen to express what is on their mind. Listen to them without interruption and try to interact with them as you would with a dear friend. Of course, I am not negating or belittling the importance of parental guidance. Sometimes, though, teens need to talk to an adult who understands and listens to them without judging them or jumping into conclusions.

This experience will show you what I mean:

> When my boys were young, there was a lot of affectionate competition between them. Matt was muscular and well built; Dru was leaner and more inclined towards his books and his chessboard. When they were young, this was not a problem, as each seemed eager to help the other when they could.
>
> At that difficult point when Dru was becoming an independent teenager, things changed. He began to bark at his brother, who used to follow him around all the time. Matt reacted in hurt confusion even though he refused to leave his brother alone. Predictably, fights began. Sometimes, they were bad enough to wear me out.
>
> One evening, after a particularly bitter spat, I took Dru with me for a walk (more so I could have some peace of mind). I was still angry, but I decided to let Dru speak so I could ease the ache between my temples. What he revealed shocked me.
>
> Dru was angry that his brother was trying to take over his personal space. He wanted to shift out of the boys' bedroom. He went so far as to say that he wanted to spend the holidays, which were just coming up, away from the family because of Matt's clingy behavior.

When I got back home, I took the boys to my favorite spot in the house, the backyard. There, we sat for a while in silence. I softly asked the boys to discuss their problems with me.

Dru was the first to respond. With a little renewed anger, Dru repeated what he told me. "I don't like Matt clinging to me all the time. He is invading my space and I want him out of my bedroom. And I want out of the holidays. I'm not going anywhere with him following me like a tomcat!"

Matt's eyes suddenly filled with tears. He was choking over the lump in his throat when he said, "I don't want to cling to you, but I don't like it when you push me away. And I want you to stay in our room. I wouldn't like it in there without you."

This answer pacified Dru a little. I slowly eased into the conversation and explained to Matt that Dru was beginning to grow up. I told him that Dru now needed a little personal space and some privacy.

"But mom, I don't want him to go away from my room. I don't like to be alone. Does this mean he will move out?"

I was about to answer in the affirmative when Dru replied, "Silly, there are no demons under the bed, you know that. And no dragons are going to get you. It's time you understood that there are no ghosts."

"Oh, I know that, but I'd still like you to be there so you can tell them to leave me alone!" came the pat reply.

We all laughed and that was the last I heard of Dru wanting to shift out. Looking back, I am glad that I took the time to listen to my sons without judging them or expressing my natural indignation. I was able to understand each of my sons better when I decided to keep silent. The same thing happened to the boys too. Once they gave up on their anger, each began to understand what the other wanted. Looking back, there are times when I wonder what would have happened if I had just taken the easier way out and interfered in the fight with my own solutions, without listening to either of them.

Listen with empathy.

Suppose your teenage daughter has been acting strange for the last couple of days. You ask her what the problem is, but she says that everything is ok. Then one day, when you are doing something together, she suddenly opens up to you.

> "You know everyone in class gets to stay out till 11 pm on Friday night. Our family rule that I have to get back before 10 p.m. is embarrassing me. Everyone laughs about it when I have to leave the group in the middle of something fun. Everyone speaks about it after I leave. Carol told me so."

How would you respond? Most parents have ready-made answers for these situations:

> "Don't worry. Stick to your position and your friends will respect you for it." "Carol told you that? What kind of a friend is she to talk behind your back? You're better off without THOSE kinds of friends." "Never mind. It's just a temporary phase. You'll soon get over it" and so forth.

Our typical response to this situation shows that we try to evaluate, judge and interpret. Then we try to affirm _our_ own decisions.

Look at this from your teen's point of view: What use is there in talking to a parent who does not seek to understand? If all you're going to get is the same old baby in a new dress, why bother?

Now imagine if you had responded in a more positive manner, like this.

> "You mean you feel like you are being pulled in opposite directions? Our family rule about time schedules is okay in itself, but when your friends poke fun at you, you feel embarrassed to leave them and run home. Is that it?"

She may agree with you and even open up some more:

> "Yes. I also feel a little afraid that I may lose my friends because I'm not too much fun if I have to rush home in the middle of a party, you know."

You will then get back to her with an understanding response like, "You feel your friends will ditch you if you leave them in the middle of your fun activities. That makes you feel scared?"

She may agree or disagree and elaborate further on what she has to share. When you respond in this fashion, you do NOT seek to evaluate, judge or evade. Your purpose is to offer a sympathetic ear – so your teen can work off their fears, insecurities and frustrations. An understanding response is one of the greatest and most effective tools in developing rapport.

Many times, listening to your child without offering any solution is a big help. By voicing their thoughts, children seek relief from whatever is eating them from the inside. They feel good about sharing with a parent, IF AND ONLY IF the parent shows a willingness to listen empathically, and give some considerations to making some adjustments. This is the easiest way to establish a deeper connection with your child.

Communicate clearly.

Did you know that communication does not mean words alone? Most people fail to understand that more than 83% of all communication is done *non-verbally*, at the subconscious level. Your words account for only 17% of what you communicate, which is really amazing considering how much we go by what we hear and say!

Your communication with your child is a complex process. When you communicate, remember your child is listening to not just your words alone, but to your tone, inflection, hand and facial gestures and you whole body language. Unless your communication is clear, you will NEVER communicate effectively, and your child will misunderstand what you mean, deliberately or otherwise.

A friend of mine once told me this interesting story:

> "I had read somewhere that little girls need lots of reassurance about their looks. I had myself grown up with a poor self-image and consequently developed complicated problems in my teens. I did not want my daughter to go through the same pain and bitterness.
>
> So I always made it a point to tell my little girl that she looked gorgeous. I wanted her to feel that she was OK. Every time I could, I always affirmed that she looked good, and I made a big fuss over whatever she wore.
>
> On one birthday, we went to a store to go shopping for clothes. There we selected a number of dresses. We were in the process of finalizing the BIG dress. I selected one dress

that I felt was particularly beautiful, but my daughter was not too happy with it. As she clutched it and looked at herself this way and that, I heard the salesperson tell my daughter, "Why don't you pick it up, honey? Your mom sure thinks you look fantastic in it!"

"Well, that's nothing new you know. She always says I look pretty, so that doesn't count."

To say that I was very shocked would have been an understatement. My daughter was only 11 years old. I did not realize that she had such an opinion about what I felt.

That put me into a few weeks of introspection. I watched and listened to myself. Sure enough, what my daughter said was true. I was so bent on reassuring her that paying her compliments had become a matter of habit with me, something I did even *without actually seeing her or looking at her.*

I understood that while my mouth was saying all the right words, many times, *my heart was not really in it.* My daughter had picked up this discord between my real thoughts and my words and decided that mom's opinions do not count."

How many times have you done the same thing? Our face says "No way!" and our words say, "We'll see."

We often say things to our children off the cuff, without considering what we are speaking about and what we really feel. Many times, it seems easy to give them the reply that they are looking for. But every time we say something we do not mean, our credibility comes down a notch.

If you want your children to trust you, then communicate what you feel. Be true to yourself. Then, communicate effectively. Look into your child's eyes and speak clearly, so that your child understands that you have put enough thought into your words. Take care that your body language supports what your words are communicating.

For instance, suppose your son wants to bring some friends over and he comes to you for permission. You are not crazy about the idea, but you don't want to break his heart. So what do you do? You say something like this, "Uhhhh...sure. I mean why not? I'd be a little busy over the weekend, but you know we could think about it over dinner. Uhhh...could you pass me that phone? I need to talk to Aunty Celine about an urgent matter."

Your words convey (vague) agreement but your body, tone and general conduct show that you are less than enthusiastic about the whole idea. Your son, like any other child, will have picked up your reluctance immediately. But since you've left the door half open, or half shut as the case may be, he broaches the subject over dinner. You may then use some other tactic to avoid a direct reply. By now, your son already knows enough to write you off!

The 'science' of communication becomes all the more important when it comes to setting limits.

If you do not communicate effectively, your child will never take you seriously. To communicate effectively, you have to be conscious of how and what you speak.

Here are a few tips to help you improve your communication with your child:

> ➢ Never say yes when you mean 'no' and vice versa.

- Always speak directly to your child, without insinuations and innuendos. If you have something to say, say it directly, in clear words. Otherwise, your innuendos may bounce off the unsuspecting head of your child without having an impact. In case your child understands your sly reference, he or she will feel insecure, insulted or confused while speaking to you.

- Never smile when you are scolding your children or rebuking them. If you smile, play and joke while you rebuke, your child won't take you seriously, and will repeat the offence.

- Do not raise your voice towards your children. If your communication is 100% effective, a quiet tone of voice and a serious expression is enough to get their attention.

- Make it clear that it is the behavior and NOT the person that is wrong. Never put a label on the person just because they repeat the wrong behavioral patterns that you disapprove.

- See that your body language supports the words you speak.

- Speak in positive terms.

A teacher once told me about a certain trend she had noticed in various classes. She said that while dealing with rebellious and tough classes, most teachers used negative language. They talked more in terms of what they did NOT want and less in terms of what they wanted. Thus, for example, if the children were talking while a lesson was going on, a teacher would say, "I do NOT want my class talking while I am teaching. Anyone who wants to talk can leave the class" or "OK, so you can't take the time to listen in class, can you? Do you think this is why you get poor grades"? This kind of language corrals the children for a little while. Yet they are back at it within a few minutes.

Now this teacher wanted to try out a new method. So every time the class misbehaved, she started speaking in terms of what she wanted. If they were talking she would say, "You know, I think we can all take a break from this lesson once we get through it quickly. However, if you disturb me, we will need that much more time to get through it, don't you think?" Or if a child forgot to bring a book, she would say, "Tom, I wish you had brought the book. This just means extra work for you since you have to copy the lesson twice."

What amazed her was that the second approach was 100% more effective than the first. Imagine that – the same message worded in a positive manner could work wonders. Try it with your children, you'll be amazed.

Stop the blame game.

Human beings are equipped with an innate desire to shift blame. We may not like it, but it's just the way we are. We have this irresistible urge to point fingers at others, even when we know deep inside that an incident could have been avoided if we had acted in a more responsible fashion.

This is particularly true about your interactions with your children. Sometimes, we police their behavior to the exclusion of everything else. Children feel threatened by this. As the saying goes, 'Offense is the best form of defense'. Children who are continually judged devise a mechanism of offense, or attack. They attack the society, their friends, teachers and parents. They blame everyone else but themselves for their lapses.

In such cases, parents need to understand that the child feels a deep sense of inner conflict. They are trying to cover up this inner conflict by shifting blame. To put an end to this behavior, it is always better to use the 'I' word in your conversation with your child.

We often catch ourselves saying 'You did this' and 'You did that' or 'How could you do such a thing'. Replace these messages with sentences like 'I feel that ...', 'I am a little concerned about this behavior' or 'The way I see it ...'.

You will notice a huge difference in your child's behavior when this simple strategy is put to work. In the first case, you are judging a person, which will inevitably lead to resistance and bad feelings.

In the second case, it seems like you are taking some amount of responsibility. 'I' conversations give the listener a feeling that they are talking to an equal, whereas accusatory sentences give an impression of the other person being inferior to the speaker.

Share a laugh with your children. Think back. When was the last time you shared a good laugh with your child? I don't mean the half-hearted here-now-gone-in-a-second laugh that parents often indulge in to pacify their children. I mean the kind of heart-warming, irresistible, inside-tickling laugh that simply breaks out and encompasses all of you in a warm bubble of good spirits.

One mother shared this experience.

> "When my children were in their preteens, I was a businesswoman working part-time from home. My kids knew that the mornings were a busy time for me. Phone calls, emails and client meetings would go on simultaneously. They all knew the unwritten family rule: Short of the house catching fire, or a stark raving lunatic invading the house, they were NOT to disturb me in the mornings.
>
> On one such busy morning, I came down from my office (that is where I worked in the mornings) to get a fresh cup of tea. When I came down, I saw my girls dancing. What caught my attention was that the two girls were dancing without a care

in the world. My eldest Alicia was teaching Amy to do a tango wearing her father's oversized T-shirt, and my high heel shoes. The sight of Alicia in those oversized tees, high heel shoes, and of Amy looking at her sister adoringly caught at my heart. Something pulled me on and I went down to the living room.

When they saw me approaching, my girls immediately stopped dancing and looked sheepish. For a moment, the three of us were quiet. Then I started dancing in a funny and exaggerated manner. Amy immediately joined in. Alicia looked surprised and stared at me with an open mouth. Then, with a giggle and a wide hug, she joined us.

That morning, I connected with my girls in a way that I have rarely done before. It was pure fun and we danced for as long as we could. Then, like a troop of giggly little girls, we all went to the kitchen and had generous helpings of ice cream.

> Humor and fun are important tools for
> establishing rapport with your child.

Humor puts everything in perspective. It stops you from taking yourself or your circumstances too seriously. Every family has its share of little things that go wrong. These minor irritants build up in the heart and hold us back. A little humor can dissolve the negative charge in a family. It can change the entire gamut of feelings permeating the family. It pulls the family closer and binds the group more tightly than before.

Age is an important factor because people who share a similar history find it easier to understand each other. So most of your rapport-problems with your child is expected and only natural. The Generation Gap, as they call it, is indeed an intimidating force that can work against rapport among parents and children.

Developing rapport with your child is an ongoing process because rapport is ever-changing. It grows, shrinks, and grows again. However, if you have a fantastic equation with your child, don't rest on your laurels yet. As the poet said, you have 'miles to go before you sleep'.

Suppose you've already beaten a path away from rapport and your relationship with your child is nothing to sing about, what can you do? If your child is unwilling to listen, cooperate or communicate with you, how can you get across the barrier?

> A sincere desire to understand your child
> is the key to building rapport.
> Remember, it is not about you. It is about them.

Don't take things personally or assume you know what they are thinking. At times, children harbor a lot of pain in their heart, that requires time and patience to get over their pain; it is *their pain*, and is real to them. They may not be ready for open communication yet. If that is so, getting frustrated or losing patience is not going to help. You may have to apologize for the pain and try to establish communication repeatedly. You will have to underline your commitment to establishing rapport by going back to your child repeatedly. It may take time but if you understand your child's deeply cherished needs for love and security, you will know that it is only a matter of time before your child opens up to you.

Remember words take up only a small percentage of the communication process. Tune into your child's feelings, look at their body language and listen to their voice, tone and inflection. These are all-important clues and will guide you to discover a lot of things that your child is not expressing through words.

Building rapport with your teen is a monumental task, and often, you may feel tempted to take the easy way out.

However, parents must NOT take the easy path to rapport.

Agreeing with your child every time is NOT the easiest way out. Allowing your child to have his or her way is NOT the best way to establish harmony. This is the escapist's route to harmony and this kind of harmony is like the calm before the storm – intransient, ominous and deadly.

As parents, we have to care enough for our children to resist and disapprove of unwarranted or damaging behavior. We simply must level with them, express our concerns and convince them of their responsibilities, and realize that it is truly up to them to make a choice. This requires a lot of courage, patience, tact and self-knowledge. A parent has to decide when to use straight talk, tact, discretion or acceptance. There may be times when shock treatment works. At other times, it can bring untold misery. There really is no thumb rule to go by. Only your heart can guide you in this matter.

It is my strong belief that children inevitably know when they are loved unconditionally. Some families slip into discord and disharmony when they take their children for granted. Children are also quick to catch this and they feel hurt and misunderstood, so there must be a continuous effort in the family to understand, ask pertinent questions, apologize, appreciate and value others.

The advantage of establishing good rapport with your children is that improved relationships with your children bring on an unusual candor and genuine warmth in family relationships. In such families, great relationships become a way of life.

Exercises

Listen

Today, take the time to talk to your child with the explicit purpose of listening only. Do not judge, evaluate or offer advice. Ask them what they like and why they like it. Become like an inquisitive child and try to speak to your child as you would with a stranger whom you like. Push all the things that you already know about your child to one corner of your mind. If you do this sincerely, I'm sure you will come across some happy surprises.

Ask your spouse or partner to watch you while you communicate with the children and spot communication glitches. Quality communication is more than just talking. Do your words carry conviction? Is your body language in sync with what you speak? Are you overly aggressive?

When your child comes to you with a problem, evaluate your first response. Is it a brush-off, a pacifier or a genuine desire to understand? Do you listen empathically? Does your child listen to your suggestions?

Speak to the members of your family about rapport and communication. Discuss body posture, body language, tone, inflection and voice modulation – these are all part of how we pay attention and listen! Discover the 'secrets' of effective communication and make it a learning experience for the entire family.

The Mirror

This is an exercise for parents. Look into the mirror and observe the way you communicate. Or if it applies, ask your partner to help you. Let them observe the way you talk. Let them observe your body language, your tone, inflection and your eyes. At the end of your talk, ask them if you came across as genuine. If not, examine those parts of your communication processes that did not measure up.

Here are certain gestures that we normally associate with aggressive behavior:

- Hands on hips
- Glaring eyes
- Arms locked in front of you
- Sitting with your legs and/or arms locked
- Turning away from a person while they are talking to you
- Looking pointedly elsewhere when someone is talking to you
- Making sounds under your breath, or sighing

These unconscious actions give you away! They speak louder than your words! Other people pick them up unconsciously and respond accordingly.

When you communicate (listen, speak) openly, try to:

- Look straight into the eyes of the other person
- Keep your body open
- Listen intently
- Ask intelligent questions to show that you are listening
- Paraphrase so you are both sure you understood correctly
- Light physical contact will establish rapport an emotional connection quickly

- → Always voice your sincere opinion; never agree just to keep the peace
- → When you speak to small children, use a gentle tone and pace your talking to match their receptivity

Establishing a connection with each of your children is essential to a happy family life. It is also one of the richest rewards of parenthood. It takes time and effort to establish that connection. Consider this: Is it not better to spend some time getting to know your child better than to suddenly face a stranger who is living with you in the same house?

Chapter 7: Handling with Care or Dealing with the Terrifying Teens

"In the life of children, there are two very clear-cut phases: before and after puberty. Before puberty, the child's personality has not yet formed and it is easier to guide its life and make it acquire specific habits of order, discipline, and work. After puberty, the personality develops impetuously and all extraneous intervention becomes odious, tyrannical and insufferable. Now it so happens that parents feel the responsibility towards their children precisely during this second period, when it is too late."

- Antonio Gramsci

Being a teen in the second millennium is a tough job. There are so many forces acting on them, pulling them this way and that. Their best friend carries a tattoo proudly on their 'unmentionables', and they are teetering dangerously on the brink of (yet) another love story. When you take a quick journey back to your own teenage years maybe 15 or 35 years ago, I'm sure you'd agree with me when I say that being a teen in the second millennium is a tough order.

Of course, the flip side of the coin is that our teens are more resilient, tougher on the inside and more worldly wise than we were. As such, they have stronger beliefs and take firm stands on issues much earlier than we probably did. 20 years ago, the tears of your mom or the heated words of your dad may have swayed you, but our teens today are compelled to stand by what they believe.

Maybe it is the fallout of super-specialization and the computer age; maybe it is because of the natural evolution that happens in every generation. Whatever the cause, the result is the same: teens today are more individualistic and more self-dependent than they were ever before. They remember that the phrase *"Yes We Can!"* echoed through the press as President Obama was sworn into office in the United States, or the Nike slogan "Just Do It".

Bridging the age gap is important while dealing with your newly emerging teen.

Your own teenage years are not a benchmark against which you evaluate your teen's behavior or the world your teen is growing up in!

Teens today are exposed to a number of issues that we never had to deal with when we were young. Our youth was the pre-Internet, pre-digital-everything era. This is the age of the Internet of Things, a media-molded and social-media-molded society! That makes all the difference!

According to popular perception, the teenage years are the time when angelic children suddenly sprout horns and fangs. I think most parents would agree. But it does not have to be so. Granted there are certain problems that are specific to teenagers, but the solution is the same as before: empathy, patience and wise parenting.

Here are some general leadership guidelines to help you transform your child's problematic teens to precious years of bonding and love:

- **Listen!** It is very easy for parents to jump the gun and assume the worst. That is the natural fallout of intense love. For the teen, nothing could be worse. Don't nag or bully your child into obedience. Listen to what they have to stay and keep the channels of communication open.

- **Facts.** Before you get judgmental or assume that your teen is on a downward spiral, check out your facts. Just because he wants a tattoo or she wants a navel ring, it does not mean that they are on drugs or are mixing with the wrong crowd. Teens often experiment with a number of surprising and adventurous behaviors as a part of growing up. After all, didn't you? They want to build their own identity and they want their new identities to be as different from yours as possible. Therefore, try to look at small incidents from their perspective. If you find that an issue is becoming too large for you to handle, make your teen understand that you need their help to deal with it.

- **Share responsibilities.** Many parents make the mistake of shielding their children from the realities of life. When something comes up, they hold hushed discussions. They do not discuss the family's financial situation with the kids or allow the children to discuss the family's money or budget. Teens are growing up and they need to feel accepted in their homes. Take them seriously and respect their views. Entrust them with adult responsibilities.

- **Rules.** Set limits and establish INVIOLABLE rules on important things like alcohol intake, cigarette smoking, dating, sexual choices and substance abuse. Discuss these vital issues with your child as early as possible. Let them know what you feel, but also allow them the freedom to confide in you.

- **Talk.** Stay involved in the life of your little adults. Know their friends and establish contacts with them and their parents.

Keep a gentle tab on what your teenager is doing in their spare time with their friends, where they go out and so on.

Handling Teen Anger

Imagine somebody screaming at you. Close your eyes and see this person. He or she is twice your size, is the person you look up to most in this world, and is your primary source of support and love. Tune in to your emotions and multiply them by 1,000. This roughly sums up what your teen feels when you scream at them.

If you share an excellent relationship with your teen, you probably know how precarious the balance is. I believe that teens bring vitality, energy and sheer fun to a family that is slowly dealing with its first mid-life crisis. They also bring in a lot of undesired and unexpected 'excitement'. For parents who share enriching and positive relationships with their teens, life can be wonderful, albeit a little unpredictable. Yet for the majority of parents, teenage is a time of great upheaval and intense emotions.

Handling anger — your own and your teen's — is one of the biggest challenges that every parent faces. Teens, with their propensity for intense emotions, can make life a roller-coaster ride for the entire family. Managing parental versus teenage anger constructively is a major challenge in most families. If anger is not handled constructively, it can poison your relationship with your child forever.

Most causes of anger are psychological. It is a rare parent who approaches his child's teenage years without anxiety. This anxiety quickly transforms itself into anger, on both sides. Most of us have been fed with enough 'propaganda' to label any misbehavior as teen behavior. We go into the relationship with perceived misconceptions. These misconceptions unconsciously rub off on our children and put them on the defensive. This sours our relationship with them, yet this is only one of the reasons for anger.

- Social isolation is one of the biggest problems faced by nuclear families today. Invariably, parents are under a lot of stress in a social scenario where one-parent families, latchkey kids, climbing divorce rates and increased mobility is the norm. Families no longer enjoy the luxury of having additional support in the form of close relatives and genuine friends. So, when rough spots develop in a relationship, parents and their teens often have no outside help to defuse the situation. Things naturally develop from bad to worse in such cases unless special and extra care is taken to rectify matters.

- Children and parents have the uncanny ability to push each other's buttons, as no one else can. As adults, are we not sometimes irrational in our relationship with our own parents? Psychologists have a name for this tendency — "ghosts from the nursery", they call it. Children trigger in us intense memories from our own childhood, in other words. This in turn causes us to react in a pre-defined manner. If you have ever wondered why your own child drives you crazy while your sister's child evokes such deep feelings of sympathy in you — this is the answer!

- Today, we do not need our teens to milk cows, run the farm or round up the cattle (usually). We may unwittingly bypass their worthy contributions just because these contributions are not necessary for survival. Teens are 'branded' in a poor light. We hear scores of painful stories about the drunken teen and the irresponsible teen, but stories of teen volunteers, social workers and responsible entrepreneurs are relatively hard to come by. Even a teen who works part-time is not given his due because his income is insignificant.

- Teens cope with major socio-political, physical, mental and emotional upheavals. Why? Because, contrary to us, in this day and age they hear about them on the Internet and via social media postings! We were not so globally aware; our children are – and it is stressful! Stress and anxiety about their immediate and greater world are major causes of teen anger and teen rebellion. Loneliness, anxiety, fear and excitement transform themselves into stress and this stress finds an outlet through anger.

- Teenage is a period of great changes within the family. While teens agonize over every new pimple, their parents spend sleepless nights over every new wrinkle! (Ah. Maybe there should be a family joke about that to ease the stress?) While teens begin to explore the new corridors of personal power opening up in front of them, parents slowly begin to accept their own limitations. While teens look forward to brighter and better opportunities, parents are dismayed by how little they have achieved. This sudden shift in the age-old paradigm of dependency between parents and their children is not to be taken lightly. Parents often find it excruciating to give up the power they once enjoyed. Knowing how and when to let go, as I mentioned earlier, is an important part of good parenting.

One father related this incident to me:

> "My daughter Eva was a bright and intelligent girl throughout her school days. She would always bring home 'A' grades. She was lively and had a passion for music. I guess we took her for granted when she was a good little girl.
>
> Our problems started when I had to relocate because of my job. This happened just as Eva started college. We shifted to

an up-market area. The college that Eva attended was well known. We knew that it had some of the wealthiest families in town. But we never thought that would be a problem for our Eva.

As before, Eva was a very popular teen in her new school. Bu this time, she somehow managed to attract the wrong crowd and started hanging out with the 'cool' kids. Sadly, we were the last to know.

Eva changed from a sweet tempered child to a stranger pretty quickly. She skipped meals, did unbelievable crash diets and shopped for the costliest items. We had huge disagreements over what she wanted to buy. Often, I had to put my foot down and refuse her.

Soon, we heard that Eva was using drugs. When we asked her about it, she was rude to us. Finally, she confirmed it. The sight of the pinpricks on our daughter's arms shattered my wife. I felt totally confused and angry. After all we had done for her, how could she do this to us? I remember thinking this classic complaint.

We talked to Eva about rehab. She adamantly refused. Things went crashing from there. I refused to speak to Eva and she acted as if she didn't care. Even so, the sight of my daughter wasting away filled me with such deep fear. Daily fights became unavoidable. At the end of these fights, Eva would leave home and stay away for days. We did not know when she would return or how long she would stay away. When she came back, she was always a little worse than before. On one such occasion, we locked her in – but she became so hysterical and violent that we had to let her out. After that, she disappeared for almost 3 months, the longest she stayed away from us.

Around that time, a new Pastor came to our local church. He heard of our problems and talked to us about Eva. He advised us to support Eva and affirm our love for her. He asked us to pray for more control. He asked us to allow the anger to seep away.

We decided to do just that. I guess we had run out of options anyway. Over the next six months, we never stopped Eva or interfered with her activities. Eva dropped out of college because she had misused the money we had given her. I still felt insanely angry – at her, our fate and at the well-meaning, sympathetic advice from friends. When things grew too difficult, I'd leave the house for solitary long walks. My wife coped better because she was not given to the same kind of rage I felt inside me.

Although it was difficult, we just accepted Eva and took care of her when she was with us. We discussed our finances and holiday plans with her as if nothing was wrong. She refused to join us for our annual holiday – another first! So we bought her some gifts when we got back. We explained to her that she would not handle the family money until she could find a way out of her problems.

After a year and a half of pure agony, we noticed some change. Eva started coming home more often. She accepted a 3-month stay at a rehab center. After coming from rehab, she took a part-time job in a nearby shop. She joined another college. This time, her grades started to improve. She had turned 18, but asked for permission to stay on until she completed her degree. We agreed.

Now, at 24, our daughter is a junior accountant with a small private firm. She recently met a young man who understands her and they seem to be making plans for the future.

I wanted to share this story with other parents out there. For us, peace came with the awareness that we had gone wrong somewhere and that the only way out was to give our daughter unconditional love.

How did we know that was the right decision? Well, a strange kind of peace and finality always accompanies the right decision. We felt that peace and we had the courage to follow what we felt was right. Anger never helps no matter how justified it is. After a point, it stops getting results and you feel more frustrated than ever."

Most families hit rock bottom when children develop indifference to the intense emotions of their parents. To handle your children effectively, a parent has to get a handle on his or her own temper and strong emotions. If your child is unafraid of your anger, he or she has been having too much of it, and has developed defenses against your anger. Swing into action and do some repair work.

The next time you get angry, do the following:

- ➢ Just before you explode, pause for a moment. Anger can never be constructive. Take it for granted that you will not be achieving anything with your ammunition. So why waste your energy?

- ➢ Once you have swallowed your anger at least a little, ask yourself some questions: What are you so furious about? Is it the misbehavior that hurts you, or your child's streak of independence? How can you change the situation? This kind of self-diagnosis is very helpful. Often, our anger at a spouse spills over and taints the relationship with our children. It helps to understand what the real cause of our anger is.

- Handle your anger in an acceptable manner. It really is OK to blow your whistle once in a rare while. Even in anger, remember you're providing a primary role model for your children, and sending a strong message that anger is "what parents do". Therefore, throwing things, name-calling and violence are taboo. Do something proactive with all that energy. Go for a run, or do a workout.

- State your expectations and set limits well in advance. Sometimes, we get angry precisely because we expect our children to adhere to rules that aren't there. If that happens, interrupt your children and calmly state what you expect.

- Avoid knee-jerk reactions. Taking some time out before you handle a delicate issue will bring you the best results. Not easy to do, particularly when you feel justified in your anger. Nevertheless, when you take some time out, you will be better able to listen and respond to your teen's side of things.

- Threats are counterproductive. We often make dire threats when we are angry, but threats become effective only when we follow through. Most parents will not have the heart to enforce what they have threatened because their threats are extreme. Empty threats will only undermine your credibility – and if you are not credible, you are not believed.

- Choose your battles. Every negative interaction with your child takes up valuable emotional resources. Focus on the larger picture, even though the little things may be driving you crazy.

Sometimes, teens get angry for apparently no reason, and who can argue with hormones! Understanding the reason behind your teen's unexplained and impetuous anger will help you deal with it in a constructive way. Here are some tips:

- ➢ When your teen is angry, do not respond in kind. Listen to them and let them vent their feelings. Once in a while, it is a good idea to allow yourself to be used as a verbal punching board for their anger. Remember they are learning how to express themselves, and need practice!

- ➢ Be empathic. Show understanding. Even if you cannot agree with them, let them know that you understand.

- ➢ Ask definite questions, "So you'd like me to allow you to party here with 10 of your friends next Sunday?" Sometimes, the reasons for anger are not apparent to us. When you do not understand what your teen wants, simply ask for a clarification, "What exactly do you want from me/us?"

- ➢ Change your attitude from "Let's fight about this" to "We are in this together". This joint problem-solving attitude promotes understanding.

- ➢ Find something to agree with when you begin your discussion. Half your teen's anger will peter out when you honestly agree with something he or she has to express. (If your kid calls you a jerk, and you agree that you are one – Wow! All the wind goes out of that sail.)

- ➢ Negotiate for a win-win agreement. "Tell you what, you can use the house provided you get the house cleaned afterwards and allow one of us to be present in the house while the party is going on."

➢ Establish standards. Make it clear to your teen that you will NOT accept violent and abusive methods of letting off steam. No hitting anyone; no picking up a weapon like a saucepan or a broom (or worse). Methods such as twisting a pillow or screaming into it, getting some alone-time, writing in a diary, going for a run or doing other physical exercise are some ways your teen can get rid of anger. (**Hint:** For your teen to follow these standards, you must stick to them yourself.)

➢ Teens often like to bait their parents so they can draw you into a destructive pattern of pointless arguments. I think it's probably true that they are actually looking for a reason to fight and take on the world. A teenager on the lookout for a fight wants nothing more than a parent who is willing to blow his or her top.

➢ Do not talk in a condescending manner or tone. Stop talking about how things were when you were younger! They don't care. Abstain from sharing pearls of wisdom. They don't care. Preaching or lecturing only provokes more hostility. Try to keep your messages concise and clear – and in the now.

➢ Express your feelings and communicate how your teen's behavior affects you. This is often a more constructive approach than direct attack. "I feel really sad about the way you talk to your sister" or "I just cannot understand why you feel that way. Help me understand why it feels that way to you."

As children grow older, they need you less and some seem to want to challenge you more and more.

This transition is particularly distressing for those parents who have put themselves wholeheartedly into parenting. So, anger is unavoidable even in the best of families, but when used constructively, it can lead to greater understanding and deeper love.

Understand that your equation with your child is changing. Evolve along with it. Diversify. Add different interests to your own life. Set aside some time to fulfill your own emotional needs. Get out more; meet people with same interests. Lastly, remember that every person has to fight his own battles. You cannot always shield and protect your child. Accept that it is OK for you to be less than perfect.

Teens and Addiction

When I was in university, 'addiction' was a shameful, dirty word – not so today! Today it is 'hip' and 'cool' to have survived a brief stint with cocaine, marijuana or crack. Peers look at you with renewed interest and possible respect. Unfortunately, the peer pressure to do drugs is probably stronger today than it was for us.

Pressure to do drugs? Respect and awe when you kick them? No wonder substance abuse is so sexy...

The distinction between abuse and addiction is slight but significant. Addiction often begins with abuse. An occasional glass of alcohol does not make you an alcoholic. However, when the alcohol becomes an integral part of a person's life in such a way that he or she cannot *function* without it, abuse changes into addiction.

People get addicted to all sorts of substances – alcohol, cigarettes, drugs, pain medication, glue, gasoline, the Internet, extreme drama and even love. The bad news is that some of these, particularly tobacco and drugs, are very addictive. Sometimes, a single incident is enough to get you hooked for life!

Addiction is the beginning of a downward spiral of destruction and waste in a child's life. Life for an addict is a haze that alters between intermittent stages of amazing highs followed by painful and depressing lows. It is also an incessant chase for maintaining the highs for as long as possible and avoiding the painful lows at any cost. In order to procure the substance of choice, children take to performing illegal acts for cash and sexual favors for the price of a fix. This puts anyone at risk for associated problems such as AIDS, prostitution, criminal charges and imprisonment, and unplanned (and unhealthy) pregnancies.

Unfortunately, by the time parents get wind of the problem, children are deep into the addiction, and chances of healing seem slim, and hope faint.

Addiction always leaves telltale signs on its victims.

Parents are often the last to know of their children's experiments with drugs and other substances.

Develop your awareness – get educated.

An alert and intelligent parent can detect the problem early if he or she looks out for the following signs:

- ➢ Sudden and drastic changes in eating habits (loss of appetite)
- ➢ Changes in sleeping habits
- ➢ Sudden weight loss, gaunt look, pallor and weakness
- ➢ Sudden and unexplained mood swings
- ➢ Propensity to withdraw into isolation
- ➢ Lack of interest in school

- Different speech patterns
- Propensity to sleep at odd hours
- Lack of mental focus
- A change in friends – some dropped; others acquired
- Disregard for curfews, schedules and deadlines, whether at home or school
- Sudden change or disregard for formerly hard-and-fast routines of any kind

Most families believe that addiction can happen to anyone but them. After all, they are loving and committed parents. They live in a healthy and happy community, and so, they deduce, there are no apparent reasons for abuse or addiction. More often than not, parents are lulled into a false sense of security. They believe that 'it can't happen to us'.

However, most parents will testify to one universal truth: all children, without exception, throw up the least expected surprises. After all, do we teach our children to lie or steal things? Even so, almost every young child goes through a phase of lying and cheating. When the offence is small, the repercussions are negligible. Children can afford to take their time in getting over it. However, in some cases – addiction, criminal activity, and sexual promiscuity, for instance – the price is too heavy to pay.

Keeping this in mind, here are certain ways and means in which parents can ensure that their child has lesser chances of falling into the addiction trap:

- Talk to your child openly about addiction, drugs and alcoholism. Educate them and yourself. Visit rehab centers with them, if possible. Give them literature to read that makes them aware of the gravity of a lapse.

➢ Keep your teen meaningfully engaged in activities they like, for example, school clubs, biking, trekking, photography, travel, adventure sports and volunteer service are constructive ways of keeping an energetic teen busy. Children who are exposed to the difficulties of life are motivated to contribute to improving the lives of others. Such children have lesser tendencies for antisocial and destructive activities.

➢ Know what is happening in your child's life. Know <u>where</u> your child is! Teens are not adults yet. Even after they cross their teen years, they are still grappling with the realities of life. They need your guidance and support, and you need to know who their friends are. And if you suspect any addictions, it is advisable to take your concerns to your family doctor and make a plan for intervention.

➢ Trust your instincts. If you develop a gut feeling that something is wrong, it probably is. Don't ignore your own gut. Parents are often so finely tuned to their children that they pick up stray signals. We are also so afraid of facing the truth and forcing an issue that we pretend not to notice.

Some of the most common causes of addiction and abuse are:

- ✓ A family history of abuse or addiction
- ✓ Low self-esteem due to unhappy and unfortunate incidents in the past
- ✓ Dangerous company; often perceived as the cool gang
- ✓ Lack of awareness of the seriousness of the problem
- ✓ Unbridled anger or self-loathing arising from negative childhood experiences
- ✓ Overindulgent parents whose only aim is to keep their children happy, no matter what

What if addiction already is a problem in your family life? Addiction can affect the entire family unit and may even pave the way for abuse problems in younger children. Thus, parents should never tolerate addicts and must get appropriate medical help for their troubled teens.

Enrolling addicts in a rehab or detox center may be the best option. A residential treatment center gives some breathing space for the rest of the family. Professional help is a must when it comes to treating addiction problems.

Teens and Sexual Awareness

Look at these startling facts:

- → 30% of teenage girls become pregnant at least once before they reach the age of twenty in the US
- → More than two-thirds of teens who have had sex regretted it and wish they had waited
- → Teens say that parents influence their decisions on sex more than any other source
- → Most teen pregnancies are unintended
- → Sexually active peers are one of the important contributing factors to teenage sexual activity
- → 21% of teen girls, and 18% of teen boys have sent a 'naughty' picture of themselves by text or email

(Source: www.teenpregnancy.org)

Let's face it – there will come a time in your teen's life when he or she is obsessed by sex. It's a natural part of life, and what with the overwhelming sexual innuendoes that the average movie-going, TV-watching child wades through, the interest is not altogether misplaced. Hormonal and physical changes in puberty awaken new feelings. Couple that with peer pressure and our age-old misconceptions ... and you have the perfect mix for sexual disaster.

Young children get their first glimpses of sexual activity from their parents. They understand what kissing, hugging and caressing is about from their parents.

Unfortunately, children also absorb new and potentially harmful knowledge from other sources like misinformed friends, the internet and trash literature. The scourge of the modern era – the Internet – has brought promiscuity into the lives of young children.

That is precisely why parents need to discuss sex with their children. If talk about sex is not encouraged at home, children will obviously turn to whatever source is available.

Young adults are curious about sex because exploring their sexual orientation is an important part of understanding who they are. Sexual awareness is a vital part of growing up.

Most parents are quick to agree that they do not want their children to become sexually active until they fully comprehend the consequences of their actions and are able to shoulder the associated responsibilities. A majority of parents feel that children should wait until their twenties before exploring physical relationships, if not waiting until marriage.

There is a reason behind this. Teen sexual activity can have dire consequences, posing significant social and emotional effects and health risks for both partners. With that in mind, parents who are willing to talk about sex in a serious yet casual manner make their child feel comfortable with the notion of sex. Remember, if it's knowledge worth having, then you are the best source to educate your child. Children who are satisfied with the knowledge they gain from bona fide sources are prepared to wait longer.

Wise decisions pertaining to sex can often make or break a child's life. Discuss the consequences of sexual behavior with your child. Most preteens already know Newton's third Law of Motion: "every action has an equal and opposite reaction". Hooking this up with realities in life is not too far-fetched. As a matter of fact, casual and concise references have more of an effect on teens than elaborate lectures. Make your child understand the consequences of a teenage pregnancy.

Discuss sexually transmitted diseases (STDs) and associated diseases. In girls, early sexual activity may lead to pre-cancerous lesions, cervical cancer or genital tract infections. In boys, early, unnatural and unprotected intercourse can lead to prostate problems and urethral infections. STDs contracted in adolescence are one of the causes for adult infertility.

I believe that educating your child appropriately about sex is one of the best ways of preventing teenage sex. Interestingly, a study published by the University of Minnesota in 2002, shows that mothers have an important role to play in their children's sexual choices. Involved mothers who communicate their values on sex make their children aware of what is right and wrong. The study showed that teens who felt 'connected' to their moms and understood that their moms were opposed to early sex often abstained from it. However, the study significantly points out that "talk alone will not get the message across".

What you can do:

- ☞ Guide your child away from hurried acts that they will regret later

- Encourage and stress the importance of high-quality education
- Empower your kids by emphasizing the value of their peer relationships and how they have more importance than "just sex"
- Set goals for the future
- Help your child develop high self-esteem
- Encourage positive and meaningful relationships with your children so they need not seek acceptance elsewhere
- Be specific about your expectations; establish precise rules and standards
- Discourage frequent and early dating
- Stay involved with your kids; know what they are reading, listening to, what they are watching.
- Know their friends and who they are hanging out with

The availability of Internet access and the sheer volume of (mis)information published on the net have complicated the work of most parents. You cannot deny access to the Internet because that's how most of us keep in touch, find more information, solve tricky problems and research the latest.

While you cannot hope to cut off your child from the Information Highway, you can set rules for smart and safe surfing. Here are certain guidelines:

- Place the computer in a room and area that is open to all; never allow your child to access the computer from a relatively private place
- Do not leave your child alone to browse
- Prohibit your child from divulging personal information on the web
- Ask them to chat only with people they know personally in a face-to-face relationship; set time limits

- ➢ When surfing the web for more information, teach your child to keep away from high-risk sites and search engines
- ➢ Discourage carrying online friendships into the real world unless they have been thoroughly checked out; establish with your child exactly what that means
- ➢ Install filters or site-blocking software on the computer so your child cannot access restricted sites

Even after you do your best to ensure safe values for your children, there are no guarantees. In the worst scenario, be prepared to support your child.

Handling Sadness, Anxiety and Depression in Teens

A client once told me this:

> "My daughter Jenna was always low on self-confidence. In school, she was perennially trying to please others. At home, she constantly blamed her brothers so she would get more love from us. We thought she'd grow out of it gradually.
>
> Now she is in high school and she's finding the going tough. She is finding it hard to get good grades. My messy divorce and her father's lack of communication after the divorce have made things worse. These days, she spends all her time in her room. Her room is always dark. She draws the curtains and just sits there in the darkness, depressed and crying. When she goes out, she wears dark and baggy clothing and covers her face with too much make-up. She doesn't talk to her friends, eats very little and sleeps all the time.

I can't go near her for fear that she will start crying. It's either that or she becomes so angry that she starts to raise her voice at me.

I just don't know how to handle her. I wonder whether she is just going through a phase or is truly depressed."

Depression is a common behavioral problem in teens.

According to a survey published in www.kidshealth.org, clinical depression affects as many as one in eight teens. It affects teens across race, color, types of family units, socio-economic status and country. Curiously, it affects females more than males.

Depression often disguises itself as sudden and unexplained mood swings. Sometimes the blues are transitory; they come and go without making a splash. However, when your child starts exhibiting radical shifts in behavior – like plunging grades, loss of weight, physical scars, prolonged lack of interest, sudden changes in eating patterns – it's time to take notice.

It doesn't take much for teens to feel extreme emotion, but don't be fooled into thinking that all teen emotion is "momentary drama". Some of the more common causes of real, prolonged depression are:

- Heredity and genetics: If it runs in the family, teens are more prone to it
- Environment
- Medical conditions
- Bitter and tragic experiences, such as a tragic death in the family
- Damaging social conditions like poverty, community sexual abuse, violence and homelessness
- Hormonal changes

- ➢ Undiagnosed learning disabilities
- ➢ Substance abuse and addiction

Parents often react to depression with anger and criticism, rather than sympathy and understanding. The inertia that accompanies depression is mistaken for lethargy or laziness. Some parents even believe that depression is all 'attitude'. This is not true. Clinical depression is a medical condition that needs immediate professional help.

How can you tell if your child has depression? Here are some of the classic _symptoms_ of depression:

- ✓ Unexplained sadness
- ✓ Inertia
- ✓ Withdrawal from family and friends
- ✓ Loss of appetite
- ✓ Sudden changes in weight and eating habits
- ✓ Inability to concentrate
- ✓ Plunging grades
- ✓ Pessimistic talk
- ✓ Talk about worthlessness, futility and suicide
- ✓ Imagined aches and pains

More than 4 of these symptoms for 3 weeks or longer may indicate depression, and **medical help should be sought immediately.**

Prolonged depression can have dire consequences. Some teens get low grades and feel that they are not up to the task of working for their grades. So they drop out of school or become irregular in attending classes. Some teens take to drugs because of depression; others take to cutting themselves, and unfortunately, some teens contemplate or attempt suicide; sadder still, some are successful.

However, there is a silver lining, if you'd like to call it that. Depression is one of the most treatable medical conditions, if diagnosed on time. Talk therapy and meditation are some of the most common forms of therapy. Sometimes doctors prescribe medicines. Engaging in group activities is also therapeutic.

> **NOTE:** Depression increases the risk of suicidal and self-damaging tendencies. Since many teens that contemplate suicide follow through (partially at least), parents who suspect depression in their teens should seek immediate medical help. Don't lull yourself into with an attitude of "She'll snap out of it."

Other Teen Problems

Clearly, the problems discussed above are only some of the most common and pressing problems faced by teens. Teens face a number of other equally pressing problems like compulsive eating, bulimia, anorexia and compulsive exercising. Most eating disorders have their roots in poor or negative body image. Unfortunately, a negative body image is the direct result of the images transmitted through the internet, TV and magazines.

With the onslaught of seductive, airbrushed body images, there is an ever-increasing hunger for the perfect bodies among teens. Sometimes parents contribute to this by talking negatively about the child or even their own bodies. A negative body image can have far-reaching effects. It can lead to:

- Poor eating habits
- Strenuous exercise regimes
- Use of dangerous and unhealthy growth supplements
- Preoccupation with food

- Overall physical illness and mental depression
- Negative self-esteem

A research published by The American Journal of Health Behavior shows that teenage girls are more prone to developing negative body image. They show a marked tendency towards developing eating disorders and food related depression. Much has been done notably by the film industry to counteract the body-image myths. Overweight and rake-thin female actors, alongside "normal-sized" actors, as well as those who "survived and recovered from" the hype of the "Hollywood body" are now speaking out to protect girls from the myth of an ideal body shape.

As teens enter the crucial phase of their life, parents need to understand the importance of positive self-image – and this for males and females alike. Here are a few tips that can help:

- Never compare your child's body – or their face – with another's
- Help your children love and appreciate their bodies – even as you the parents do the same for yourselves
- Do not speak ill of your own body
- Develop a healthy and balanced lifestyle
- Opt for healthy food choices
- Exercise regularly
- Educate your child about the use of cosmetics
- Speak to your child and understand their fears
- Encourage your child to explore ways of appearing attractive, like dressing well and appearing neat
- Stress the importance of developing a beautiful mind

Preteen and teenage years are a period of conflicting emotions and unexpected growth. Your teen is the same adorable child who sat in your lap holding your fingers and listening to you in rapt attention.

The only difference is that he or she has now developed that same all-encompassing wonder for the world outside. Your teen has to practically learn the ropes of independent life in these few problematic years. There is tremendous pressure on them to grow up, do well and toe the line. It is time to let them wander away from you and explore the limits of the world. You only have to extend a gentle guiding hand to keep them within limits and they will eventually grow up into lovable, loving and responsible adults.

Chapter 8: At the Potter's Wheel

"Your children are not your children. They are the sons and daughters of Life's longing for itself.

They come through you but not from you, and though they are with you, yet they belong not to you.

You may give them your love but not your thoughts, for they have their own thoughts.

You may house their bodies but not their souls, for their souls dwell in the house of tomorrow, which you cannot visit, not even in your dreams.

You may strive to be like them, but seek not to make them like you. For life goes not backward nor tarries with yesterday."

— Kahlil Gibran

This poem has always touched me deeply. How true these words are if you look at our roles as parents from a philosophical point of view!

As parents, our duty is to mold our children, just as a potter molds his pot at the potter's wheel.

Our children are like works of art, although our job as parents never truly ends. Consciously or otherwise, we model our children after ourselves throughout our lives. Every child is a unique challenge and every moment you spend with your children is an opportunity to teach, share and lead. Whether we teach the right lessons or the wrong is up to us, and sometimes we do make 'mistakes'.

A woman in her mid-fifties once shared her fears with me.

> She was deeply troubled by her young son's inclination to splurge. He was a hard-working young man, who wanted to save for his college education by working part-time at the local restaurant. But after he started earning, he changed. He started spending whatever he earned on electronic gadgets, CDs and trendy watches. By the end of each month, the young man was living off his credit cards.
>
> A little talk between us revealed two interesting facts: the boy's father was an executive who was denied a car loan in the past, because he had bad credit. His mom – the woman I was talking to – had just spent a good part of her monthly salary on two new suits!

How can you expect your child to travel a path different from the one you're walking on?

> *There are a number of things that a teen needs to learn, and they won't be learning those*

from schools or textbooks.
They learn it by observing life.

They imbibe most of it from you and some of it from the influences around them.

Our first duty as parents is to become the kind of person we want our kids to be. Not easy, but essential!

Our next duty is to equip our children to lead a happy and well-adjusted life. Many of us believe we are doing just that, but are we really giving our teens the kind of leadership and knowledge they need?

Think about your teenage years for a moment — when you started work, were you prepared for life? I'd say not, unless you had parents with lots of foresight! The truth is, some of us have messed up our early years because we did not have the soft skills to survive. Some of us may still be paying for it!

You need to teach your teen basic survival skills because these skills are vital to their adult life. Most of us have learnt these skills the hard way. We have come to take them for granted. But, ask yourself this, if you knew some of the lessons that you learnt in your 30s when you were 18, wouldn't it have made life easier for you? By passing on your accumulated wisdom, you will be arming your child with important coping and survival skills.

Talk with your teenager, talk to them, do your best to pass on the lessons you have learned. Once you have talked to your child about a skill and shown them how it's done, allow your child to do it a few times under supervision. From then on, trust children to do the task on their own. They may make mistakes, but hey, better to make mistakes when they are still under your wings than when they are all alone in the world, don't you think?

Money Management

Managing cash, credit cards and bank accounts, are some of the most critical survival skills we need as adults. In recent years, talk of money had become impolite and unfashionable. However, with the economy changes, and jobs being threatened, it is time to break out the serious discussions on financial health and responsibility. When teens get their first part-time job, everyone in the family is excited. However, if you have not taught your teen the right money-management skills, that first job, and others following it, could still have them looking to you for financial support.

Some of the important lessons in managing money that every child needs to learn are:

- **Saving.** There is only one-way to financial freedom – to spend less than you earn. In theory, this seems such a simple lesson, but practicing it can be difficult, even for adults. From a young age, teach your child to earn his rewards. If they want a new shoes or a phone , ask them to earn a percentage of its cost. This will make your teen understand the value of money and the need to save.
- **Frugality.** This is something that children learn automatically from parents who show a healthy respect for money. Shopping around for the best deals, taking proper care of their belongings so they get maximum benefit of their money, settling for cheaper options and controlling impulsive buying are some important lessons in thriftiness. Parents who constantly eat food from expensive places, go on shopping sprees at the drop of a hat and spend like there's no tomorrow when there is no money in their bank to pay the bills, are begging their kids to follow the same path.
- **Credit management.** According to various surveys, teens and young adults make up the largest share of credit card holders

in America. Young adults exposed to the dazzling but tricky world of credit cards take hasty decisions that cost them dearly in later life. Talk to your teens about the responsible use of credit. Tell them how important it is to avoid debt. As they say, 'the bold print giveth and the fine print taketh away'. Teach your teenager to read the fine print.

- **Investing wisely.** All right. You have money. What good is it going to do you, though, if it is just sitting in the bank? Teach your child how to research and invest. Teach them to look for ways to make money replicate itself.
- **Giving back.** Charitable giving and volunteerism, whether it is support by offering your money or your time, can do a whole lot for both your family and your teen.

Managing finances is vital to a successful life. The sooner your child learns it, the better equipped they are to making their fortune, or at least staying above water. The above is a quick listing of the most important money-management skills your teen needs to develop.

If you wish to teach your child the practical details of making money and getting wealthy, you may need a more comprehensive guide. With the Internet explosion in our lives, making money can be a whole lot easier than it has been in the past. Losing money is easier still. Fortunately, you can help your child manage their pennies and dollars. All you need is a little know-how.

With my daughter's help, I have written a book that aims to teach teenagers the secrets of handling and making money. The book is a practical guide with lots of tips and tricks. The book is '*The Wealthy Teen...A Guide for Parents Teens and Mentors*' and you can order a copy from my website, www.thewealthyteen.com. Carly's input was essential to the writing of this book because through her ideas, I could touch upon the skills that teens possess and the requirements that they most respond to.

Extracurricular Activities

How good are extracurricular activities? "Oh, my teenage daughter just doesn't have the time to do anything. After classes, she goes for art lessons. Then, she is off to karate classes. In the evenings, she works part-time at a library. On weekends, she goes for special piano classes. She's learning a lot. I'm so proud of her".

Teens come in all varieties. Some parents complain that they need to push their teens off the couch and force them outdoors for fresh air and exercise. Others feel the need to curb the adrenalin of sports-crazy teens, and still others have to bridle the enthusiasm of their over-achievers so they do not burn out. It is all very well to expose your teens to a variety of skill sets. By absorbing more skills, your teen's personality will flourish, the rough edges will disappear and a well-rounded individual will surface.

Nevertheless, there is a growing belief that student life is a frantic rush to attaining as much expertise in as many streams of knowledge as possible. People believe that the more your teens achieve, the happier they'll be. Some parents place a great deal of pressure on their teens to get involved in a number of impressive and highly taxing extracurricular activities. Of course, the intentions are noble. Parents know how important it is to present an impressive array of extra skills in their teen's college applications. But those teens who take up activities at gunpoint seldom get anything positive out of their experience. In the end, all the time and effort they put into that particular activity is a waste. Teens should engage in extracurricular activities primarily for the pleasure it offers them, and secondary for the discipline it gives them.

Today, the teen's world is a mad rush to keep pace. They keep running from pillar to post, having accomplished a lot on paper and nothing in particular. The term 'extracurricular' is meant to denote a side-activity that is relaxing and pleasurable to the mind. If teens learn to relax and enjoy what they do, they will be healthier and happier adults.

Please don't get me wrong; I have nothing against extracurricular activities. Nevertheless, some spare time (down time) is important to the health of your teenager. It is how they recharge. Listening to an ear-shattering dose of heavy metal may not seem like relaxation to you, yet for some, it is what they need to unwind.

If your child does not relate to running behind a ball like their life depended on it, don't force them to participate. Look for something else. That may break your heart, but it's your child's life, not yours. While sport activities are edifying, they are not the only beneficial activities around. Participating in volunteer organizations, or church functions, teaches teens about a world bigger and more diverse than their own. Most of these activities are good for the heart and soul and they offer important life-lessons that a young adult can easily pick up. Extra activities can offer your teen the opportunity to learn how to be a good team player, discipline through practice, how to take care of equipment, how to deal with disappointment, how to be a good sport, how to make and accomplish goals, and develop attributes that will serve them well in the years to come.

Music, drama and art are some wonderfully creative activities. Theatre and reading groups can be fun. Debating classes can help bring out the spokesperson in your teen. All of these teach your teen to express themselves in a better fashion. Then, there are certain activities, like trekking and camping, which are great exercise, and pure fun, indulged in for fun's sake.

Whatever activity your teen decides upon, moderation is the watchword. You are still the parent and you are in control. Activities that monopolize your teen continually should be avoided.

Mind Management

<u>Positive thinking</u> is one of the most important life skills we must teach our youngsters before they get ready to take on the world. According to the National Institutes of Health, 1 in 8 adolescents may be suffering from acute depression. The world we live in is so full of negative feedback that we need to arm our children with the tools to fight it, and stay focused on their path.

While all our curriculums emphasize the importance of critical thinking, positive thinking is left out of the pail. Of course, one of the best ways of inculcating positive thinking is by leading the way. Children learn what they observe. If you live your life like a thundercloud ready to burst, don't be surprised to hear your teen make dire prophecies about the end of the world.

Start presenting your own thoughts in a positive manner. 'Oh well, seems like I've misplaced my house key. We'll just have to go back to the grocery store to see if it has been found there!' This will let your child know that a minor slip-up is not the end of the world. They will also learn to look for alternative solutions in a calm manner.

Keep a cheerful smile on your face and a happy thought in your mind. Eventually, your child too will learn the power of positive thinking. As Mary Kay Ash, the famous founder of Mary Kay Cosmetics was known to say, "Fake it till you make it".

<u>Self-motivation</u> is another important skill that the growing teen needs. Motivation starts with a desire, a dream and a need to fulfill something. Parents who maintain performance charts at home, offer small treats and outings as rewards for desired behavior are teaching their children about motivation.

Teens who lack motivation start exhibiting homework problems which may develop into greater difficulties as they grow. Depression, lack of energy, hopelessness and unreasonable anger can happen when there is no motivation.

Motivate your child instead of giving them ultimatums. While ultimatums wear off, motivation only increases the urge to achieve. Rewarding positive behavior is one of the best methods of motivation. On the other hand, punishing undesired behavior can actually kill the motivation to excel.

Goal Setting

There is an old story about a young man in a foreign land.

> As he walked through the unfamiliar roads, he came upon an old man, who looked like a sage.
>
> The young man asked, "Where does this road lead to?"
>
> "Where do you want to go?" The old man asked in return.
>
> "I don't really know", mumbled the perplexed young man.
>
> "In that case, what difference does it make where this road leads to?" the old man asked with all the wisdom of his years.

As teens develop into young adults, responsibilities begin piling up. The pressure to excel goes up and a thin line demarcates success from failure. In the overly competitive state of affairs we see around us, successful goal setting is a vital key to success.

Goals are dreams with an action plan and a deadline. When dreams are defined in terms of actions, they become goals. For example, you may dream of owning a car. It is only from the moment you start calculating the amount of money you need and writing down the ways and means of making that money, that your dream becomes a goal.

Of course, all of us have goals, but how many of us fulfill them? Some of us make New Year's resolutions, and how many of us follow through? When our own records are so dismal, how can our teens learn better? Goal setting is a vital success tool. Help your child feel the thrill of achieving goals. Here are some practical tips that will make it easier for your child to set and meet goals.

- ✓ Set specific goals: Something like 'I'm going to behave better' is not a specific goal. It will not work. Behave better in what way? By getting up early, changing your food habits, controlling your anger – what? People who succeed with goal setting make specific goals like 'I'm going to read 20 pages of a novel every morning.'

- ✓ Set short-term goals first: Short-term goals should lead to long-term goals. For instance, suppose your long-term goal is to pass an exam, chunk it down into short-term goals, like so:

    - Study every day for 1 hour
    - Pass every class test in that subject
    - Do some extra reference work in that subject
    - Make quizzes to test my knowledge

    If you meet these short-term goals, you will automatically meet your long-term goal of passing the exam. Short-term goals must have a start and finish date. This definite time-span is vital to the success of short-term goals.

- ✓ **Set achievable goals:** If your teen has just started training for soccer, they cannot realistically hope to qualify for the national team in a year. To work, goals must be challenging, but not out of reach.

- ✓ **Goalposts help success:** Knowing what they have to achieve each day keeps the child motivated. At first, parents can help break down activities into smaller bits. Soon, your teen will learn this art themselves.

- ✓ **The power of repetition:** Teach your teen the power of repetition. You cannot set a goal and expect things to work out automatically. In most cases, meeting a goal is often the result of changing certain behavioral patterns or learning new and more effective ones. If your teen wants to lose weight, they will have to adapt to a new pattern of healthy eating. Behavioral changes are not easily accomplished, so one has to learn the techniques of making a goal 'stick'. Saying your goal out loud while looking into the mirror or writing it down and taping to a door, are some of the ways in which your teen can remind themselves of the goal. Remember, the more a goal 'sticks', the greater its impact.

- ✓ **Perseverance pays:** Let's accept it – goals are difficult things to achieve. That is why you have nine people running after the ball in soccer! Seriously, goals do take time and an iron will. Ask your teen to be prepared for slippage; slippage just means they didn't keep to some part of their decision. Teach them that they must learn to pick themselves up every time they fall. Teach them to get back on track every time they fall off.

Many people, including teens, do not set goals because of certain factors:

- Fear of failure: 'What if I don't make it?'

- Fear of success: 'Heck, what if I make it? Can I handle it?' You may not believe it, but many of us are actually *afraid* of getting what we want!

- Lack of motivation: 'Dad wants me to save the money I make. Why should I? It's my money.' Limited thinking is one of the reasons behind this lack of motivation.

- Procrastination: 'Well, I'll watch TV today and start my work tomorrow.'

- Lack of information: When you don't know how important your goals are, you will never set them or meet them. A teen who does not understand why it is important to excel in education is never going to set serious goals about his or her education.

- Lack of awareness: Goal setting, like other tools for self-improvement, is a science. There is a method to it. Ignorance of these rules and guidelines will make it almost impossible to set or meet realistic goals.

Reward is an important part of goal setting; it is also the part that we most overlook. Every time your teen achieves a short-term goal, praise them and have a small celebration. Celebrate in whatever way that makes your teen happy. This sense of accomplishment is important to keeping motivation levels high.

Time Management

As children reach their teenage years, their calendars begin to fill up rather rapidly. Assignments, studies, extracurricular activities, a part-time job and a hectic social life can take its toll on your teen if they do not know how to manage their time efficiently.

As an adult you know that time is one of your most important resources. You also know that everybody has only 24 hours in a day. How you make use of your allotted quota of time decides how successful you are in juggling your various activities. This applies to your teen also.

Here are certain tips that will help your teen manage their time in an effective manner:

- → Put it down in black and white: The first step in time management is to find out how your time is being utilized right now. Help your teen fill an hourly chart of activities for one week. This kind of a chart will often act as an eye-opener. Your teen may be surprised at the amount of time leaking away through telephone chats, watching television, being on the internet, or partying with friends ... or traveling in town. Once they discover how their time is being utilized on an hourly basis, they will be able to decide what activities to cut down on.

- → Prioritize: Make your teen understand that they cannot do everything at once. Your teen should be able to pick and choose the activities that are important. Limiting your teen to one or two activities this week is probably a good idea to start off with.

- Set up a schedule: When activities begin to pile up, it is easy for teens to lose their nerve and give up in frustration. Add an unexpected event like a bad cold or a surprise visit from a relative, and it might seem as if everything is ready to burst at the seams. To avoid stress and to get things done on time, set up a schedule. Set aside a particular number of hours for every activity, leaving some extra room for unexpected delays. You'll be surprised at how easy things become once you know exactly what you have to do and when you have to do it. Reward your teen for sticking to their schedule.

- Get organized: Every parent will probably agree that their teen spends endless hours searching for one thing or the other. You'll be amazed at how much time you could save when you know exactly where your stuff is. Teach your teen to keep all their valuables, tools, keys, clothes, money and personal stuff in a place where they can find it easily.

- Take the plunge: This is an important step in time management. Many times, young adults prepare elaborate timetables and schedules, only to sit back and admire their handiwork. Occasionally, they may even be a little overwhelmed by the tasks ahead. In the end, they may spend a day or two dawdling and making plans. However, procrastination gets you nowhere. Help your teen understand that planning is no good if it is not followed by action.

- Get rid of the attitude: I often come across parents who unwittingly dampen the enthusiasm of their teenagers in their pursuit for perfection. Understand that when your child has too many roles to perform, what matters is not perfection but satisfaction. Allow yourself to be guided by how your teen feels.

→ Chill out: Your teen is still a young person. Yawning in class, glazed eyes at the dinner table and a general lack of enthusiasm can only point to one thing: lack of rest. Encourage your teen to find enough time for a sound sleep, entertainment and fun activities.

Social Skills

Do you know any adults about whom you'd say, "He/she has no social graces"? Most of us know more than one!

These skills might seem obvious. After all, do we really need to learn to share and love one another? Teach your teen the importance of being compassionate, thoughtful, loving and giving, better yet, set the example for them to follow.

Teach your children to be good conversationalists. A good conversationalist is not a person who can captivate the audience with their sparkling wit. To be a good conversationalist, one has to be a good listener, and know how to ask a leading question or two. Teach your teen to listen to a conversation with interest. Teach them to react in an appropriate fashion.

Values like courtesy, etiquette and proper manners are learnt automatically through emulation of the adult world. However, talking about them will make your teen more aware of the necessity to develop these qualities. I know of one thoughtful dad that purchased an etiquette book, and spent an afternoon with his son and son in law, going through the book pointing out social graces.

Eating Habits

Soda, pizza, French fries, carbonated drinks, chips, chocolate bars and burgers form the staple food of many teens today. While a national controversy rages over the causes of teen obesity and obesity related diseases, our teens continue to munch from fat-filled, high calorie packets.

Weight issues matter a lot to your teen. These days when everybody wants to sport beach board abs and jutting collarbones, fat does matter. So it's no use trying to tell your child that it is just baby fat. Help your teen regulate their food habits from the very beginning.

"Lunch for me is fries, soda and an ice cream. That's all I like to eat," says Terry Bright, a 15-year old studying in high school. Now, all around the world, schools are actively involved in spreading a heightened awareness of healthy eating. Still, change is something very hard to come by, as many schools are discovering. Even when there is a ban on unhealthy fast food, teens simply sneak off campus to get what they can't find in their lunchroom.

Teenage obesity has been linked to a host of health problems and eating disorders. Parents, who worry about weightier issues like teen pregnancy and drug abuse, often do not have the heart to pick a fight over a bag of chips. However, this permissive attitude only exacerbates the issue.

Conscious parents raise self-aware teens. It helps to be conscious of the factors that lead to teenage obesity:

- → Genetic factors
- → Overeating
- → Emotional eating
- → Lack of exercise

- → Overdose of fast food
- → Hormonal changes
- → Lack of sleep

While these factors may lead to obesity, there are more pressing reasons for our children becoming overweight.

Unhealthy eating in teens happen due to a number of reasons.

- ➢ Grab 'n' go: some teens are lazy about food and prefer to grab what they can see already prepared, rather than eating something they have to make. Teens who are always on the run like quick solutions. There's nothing easier than chewing a bar of chocolate or downing a bottle of soda for lunch. Help your teens eat right by cutting fresh fruit and vegetables and leaving it on the table where they can see it, or in the fridge, ready for them to grab as a fast snack.

- ➢ Convenience: Most working parents cannot find time to pack a healthy lunch for themselves or their children. A teen armed with money is spoiled for choices when they reach the school cafeteria.

- ➢ Make them aware: Teens are often confused about fat content and calorie intake. In their bid to lose weight, they often end up eating the very things they should avoid. Many sugared foods billed as fat-free have a lot of calories. For instance, when your teen opts for a huge bowl of fat-free pasta, they are not aware of the empty calories that are going in. Their body breaks down the food and says 'I don't need all these calories right now, so I'm going to store it all away as fat'. Making your teens aware of the fat-calorie relationship is one of the most important tools you can give your child.

> Make way for the new chef: With the focus on cooking shows on TV, ask your teen to cook a healthy meal that they have seen on TV, or make one night a week a family cooking night where all participate in the meal preparation.

> Teach your teen the importance of moderate and consistent exercise. This one is difficult. Believe me, I speak from experience. Although I exercise regularly and speak to my children about the importance of regular physical activity, it is difficult to get through during those hectic teen-years. However, persistent effort often pays off. In the very least, it will keep your children away from unhealthy weight management plans like purging or over exercising.

Most teens begin aggressive dieting in order to curb their real or perceived weight problems. Surveys show that teens have a predisposition to select fad diets. This is probably because of media exposure and peer pressure. Whatever the reasons, attempts to lose weight without much effort can only lead to depression, frustration and sickness.

Happiness Skills

For some reason, this is one skill that we forget to teach our children: How to be happy. We simply assume that when they have everything else they need, they will automatically find a way to happiness. Sadly, this is not the case.

✓ Teach your teens to enjoy their present moment. This is a skill that younger children automatically have. However, as they grow up into teens and young adults, people start thinking about their past and their future. Inevitably, the present slips away. Living for the future or living in the past is a matter of habit. Happiness comes when we learn to live in the present while preparing for the future from lessons learnt in the past.

- ✓ Help your teens find a purpose in their lives. It could be something ordinary, like getting a particular job or qualifying for something or finding your calling. It could even be a higher religious purpose. Whatever it is, having a purpose to work towards is extremely important in life.

- ✓ Talk to your teens about the importance of developing lasting relationships. To some extent, children automatically pick it up from your relationship with your spouse. Teach your teens that bumps are part of every relationship and equip them to smooth out bad patches with the right skills of communication, compromise and empathy.

- ✓ Help your teens find the courage to say 'no'. Teens face many situations where they may feel they need to do something risky, unhealthy or downright harmful just so they could get along with their peer group. Unfortunately, many teens end up doing things that they should not simply because they are afraid of losing a friend or being left out of the crowd. The trick is to teach your child to say 'no' in a variety of ways so they can handle tricky situations with finesse.

Teach them to:

- Use humor to divert attention and lighten a situation
- Explain the rationale behind their decision to do or avoid something
- Pretend as if they have not heard something; sometimes, acting as if you haven't heard something is the best way to deflect an undesirable action

- Say no and stick to their decision; children have to be trained to say no in the firm and authoritative manner; half-hearted refusals may end up in compliance
- Leave the scene of an undesired situation; teach your teen to have the courage to leave a situation that has the potential to turn negative; if they lead the way, other teens who do not want to be there will also follow them

In addition to the above, teens also need to be exposed to a lot of practical knowledge. Why things work and how things work and how to take care of things are some important pieces of knowledge.

We often see parents cooking, cleaning, washing, arranging and organizing for their teens. Many parents talk about the need to develop these skills but never allow their teens an opportunity to gain practical knowledge. Teach your child to live in a clean, uncluttered and organized manner.

Teach your teen practical life-skills. How to keep things in working order, how to fix things around the house and how to use their logical problem-solving skills are important pieces of knowledge. Teens who grow up with skills in plumbing, heating, painting, electricity and roofing, among other things, naturally become more aware of the world around them. The point is to expose your child to life in all its glory. Let them see the rough edges and taste the smooth. This helps them acquire balance.

Conclusion

*"There are only two lasting bequests we can hope to give our children.
One of these is roots, the other, wings."*
- Johann Wolfgang von Goethe

We don't think about it much in the delightful times of our new-born getting stronger and bigger. They cannot talk yet, or move around enough to get into trouble. Our child is The Cutest Little Kid, and we are not yet too fraught with the challenges of parenting – aside from getting too little sleep!

That soon changes, as if overnight. It isn't overnight, and, yes, I agree – the teen years arrive far too quickly! We parents can go from being the younger kids' heroes to being our teenagers' enemy. From being seen as really smart to being considered really, really dumb. We move from being the go-to person to being the run-from person in their lives!

The teenage daughter of a friend had a name for all adults. 'Snoopervisor' was the official term and what it means is pretty obvious!

Teenage years can be a difficult time for all parties involved. It is a period of intense push and pull, power struggles, overwhelming emotions and knee-jerk reactions. It's one helluva ride ahead and you'd better keep your seat belts fastened tight!

To me, the shining light at the end of the tunnel has always been a broad vision of what my children will grow up into. I have always found great relief in keeping that picture in front of me and working towards that goal. I do believe that parents who are able to do this develop the ability to overlook temporary problems and minor mishaps. They are also able to provide a non-intrusive and gentle helping hand when their kids stray from the path.

Listen. Talk. Repeat.

One of the most powerful tools we have as leaders of our children is the power of open clear and loving communication. You see, children WANT to be loved, accepted and cherished, no matter what their age. They want to be accepted for who they are not for who their parents want them to be.

When you explain to your teen your thinking processes, your fears and your reasons, many of them will understand. There is no shame in explaining to your teen that your decisions need not always be correct, but they are the best you can deliver. Explain that everything you advocate, advise and demand is directed towards moving your teen to safety and happiness. Admit to your great love for your child and make them see that a big part of your happiness depends on their well-being.

Tell your teenager that every parent hopes for the very best for their children. From years of experience, we see the potholes on the road and we want to protect our teens from falling in. We warn them, challenge them and nag them because we have their greater interests in mind. Accept in your heart that you cannot always protect your teenager from harm. First of all, you are not always going to be there. Second of all, some of life's lessons are better learnt after a good bruise. Allow them the freedom of choice and the thrill of experimentation. And take them in, warmly, when they finally find their way home.

As they grow older, your teens will inevitably find themselves at tight corners. Being at a party where alcohol, drugs, cigarettes and sex flow freely is quite possible. Your teen could be poised precariously at the edge of temptation and succumbing to an addictive drug. Your child may be pressured into joining a gang, or may secretly wish to enjoy the thrill of raw power. These are all situations that you wish you could expunge. Unfortunately, it doesn't work that way. As children spread their wings, parenting is less about exercising control and more about offering direction. You can only show them the way to happiness, as you are in pursuit of your own.

> *"Parents need to grow and develop immense maturity as their children grow. This crucial change sometimes never happens. While our kids grow up from toddlers to preschoolers and then into teens, we are still stuck with the picture of the boy or girl who accepted us beyond all expectations. But that's not how it works."*
>
> Dr. Mitch Gabel, clinical psychologist

The guidance we give our children has to answer their needs. You see, the grown-up teen in front of you is NOT the same boy or girl you remember of 10 years ago. They have changed in ways that you may not even know.

Yes, there are indescribable challenges on the way. There will be tears, anger, bitterness and pain, but I believe that in spite of all the struggles that are inherent in family life, every trial you face is worth it. There is a rich reward in seeing your child go out into the world and conquer it in their own way. There is an inexpressible pride in seeing a part of you live life in a different way. Then, there is that unutterable joy in looking into faces that still remind you of the time you wiped a tear away, helped them walk, watched them eat spaghetti, or their first birthday cake. If there is pain and sadness in the present, there is immeasurable joy and satisfaction in the future.

We each have a wealth of opportunities to improve our parenting – and to improve ourselves. The secret of successful leading as a parent is to keep the faith and to keep forging ahead in spite of setbacks. We never know which final push will catapult our children to the path of truth, happiness and freedom.

Wishing you all the best with your wealth of parenting opportunities!

Post Script

"Parenthood remains the greatest single preserve of the amateur."

– Alvin Toffler

Don't despair – even amateurs can get quite good at their hobby! Parenthood is an adventure. A learning opportunity. The source of a wealth of frustration ... and of love, pride and satisfaction.

If you don't believe me, wait for grand-parenthood. I am willing to bet you'll be ready to do it all again ... but still be relieved that you can send those grand-kids of yours back home to their own parents!

If you have any parenting stories you would like to share, please go to www.thewealthyteen.com to email them to me. Also look to this site for further information on "The Wealthy Teen – A Guide for Teens, Parents and Mentors", which is a workbook designed to deliver practical tips and techniques for building great money habits.

Made in the USA
Lexington, KY
16 September 2016